The New Sermon Slot (Year

C000139453

Sharon Swain is a former teacher and Diocesan Adviser ~~~~~~~ ~~~~~
education to the Diocese of Worcester. She has three rural churches, and is
the Diocesan Evangelism Adviser. She is the author of several highly
successful SPCK books, including *Conversations with God*, the two *Christian
Assemblies for All-Age Worship – Years 1 and 2*, and *The New Sermon Slot:
All-Age Ideas for the Common Worship Lectionary (Year B)*.

This book is dedicated to David and Wendy Steventon
for all their help and kindness

THE NEW SERMON SLOT

All-Age Ideas
for the Common Worship Lectionary
(Year C)

SHARON SWAIN

First published in Great Britain in 2000
Society for Promoting Christian Knowledge
Holy Trinity Church
Marylebone Road
London NW1 4DU

British Library Cataloguing-in-Publication Data

A catalogue record for this book is available from the British Library

ISBN 0–281–05191–7

Typeset by Wilmaset Ltd, Birkenhead, Wirral
Printed in Great Britain by
The Cromwell Press, Trowbridge, Wiltshire

Contents

INTRODUCTION

The New Sermon Slot (Year C), like *The New Sermon Slot (Year B)*, is based on the Common Worship Lectionary three-year cycle of readings used by many churches. It aims to give those who are responsible for organizing all-age worship some suggestions for incorporation into the normal framework of their service, as part of the Service of the Word within the Communion Service, or the 'sermon slot' in the Family Service.

The book allows for a wide variety of situations, and encourages leaders to tailor the suggestions to suit their own individual needs. The ideas are based on the readings in Year C of the Common Worship Lectionary, allowing leaders to adapt them to suit their circumstances in a practical way, whether that is for adults and children, or adults alone. *The New Sermon Slot* is primarily a book of practical suggestions that allows worship leaders to expound more fully the word of God. Some notes are included for leaders to enable them to add a comment, and these can be expanded to suit local circumstances.

☐ *The Family Service*

The 'family' or 'all-age' service reminds us that we are all on a journey of pilgrimage together. Children and adults need each other to progress along the path, and to learn and worship apart can hinder their progress.

The traditional family service must no longer be a children's service, or indeed a time when the church pays lip service to its children. The family service, whether it is eucharistic or not, must take account of all ages in the church.

The organizers of the family service face a challenge to occupy the adults' minds (and often, though not always, their maturer understanding of the faith), as well as the children's desire to worship with their whole body.

The New Sermon Slot gives ideas for those faced with the challenges of conducting all-age services. It uses the traditional teaching point of the service to allow congregations to stop and look at the message of Jesus Christ and at their response.

☐ *The All-Age Service*

For those who wish to get the most out of this book the following suggestions might be helpful:

- All-age services need a *team* of people to organize them. Do not expect one person to do it all.
- All-age services need *advance planning* and *prayers*. Think and plan at least four or five weeks ahead to get the best out of the service.

- All-age services must be *flexible*. Anything can – and often does – happen when those who take the service are using modern methods of education. You may also need to tailor the instructions to suit your circumstances, and double the number of groups or dispense with some. But with the Holy Spirit's help, and good planning, even difficulties can be turned to your benefit.
- All-age services are for *everyone*. You cannot always keep the two-year-old occupied and neither should you expect to all the time, but there should be something for every age in the service.
- All-age services are for *equals*. Never talk down to children or new adults in church. They may know more than you, or be spiritual giants. Equally, don't expect those who have been worshipping for 50 years to know all the answers, for they won't. In the all-age service all are equals!
- The reason for learning in such a practical and experiential way is not about 'getting back to childhood'. It is important everyone has the opportunity to learn more about their faith, and we learn best by what we see, hear *and* do!
- All-age services need the *goodwill* of some people. If flak occurs don't give in, but do question whether you went too fast at first. Don't threaten anyone by asking them direct questions, or by making them take part. Take things slowly and don't try to change everything overnight.
- All-age services are *fun*. Learning about God can be fun as well as instructive. So enjoy yourself.

Note: The text of the New RSV Anglicized edition has been used throughout the book, except on pages 93–4 where the text is from the Jerusalem Bible.

THE FIRST SUNDAY OF ADVENT

Christians know that God's kingdom will one day be established throughout the world. This week we explore the notion of a just kingdom.

Jeremiah 33.14–16
1 Thessalonians 3.9–13
Luke 21.25–36

- Group leaders.
- Newspapers.
- Frieze paper.
- Prit-tak or drawing pins.
- Paint (Optional: collage materials).
- Pencils.
- Suitable paper (e.g. gold or silver) to make crowns.
- Scissors.
- Paper.
- Stapler or glue.
- Paper or plastic to put under Group 3's work.
- Old shirts.

□ *Comment*

Jeremiah speaks of a time when God's people will be gathered up from across the world, wherever they have been scattered, so that he can create a new kingdom. He will establish a king of his choosing, one who will be a righteous king, and who will lead his people in the way that God wants.

St Paul, in the New Testament reading, picks up this same theme. He writes of the new kingdom brought in by Jesus. We have been saved from a kingdom of darkness, and transferred into a kingdom of light ruled by God's son, Jesus Christ. Through Jesus we have been redeemed and bought back from slavery. Through Jesus our sins have been forgiven, and we have been reconciled once more to God. Moreover Jesus, who is the head of the church, is also the image of God. Through him everything in the world has been made. He is in fact the King above all kings, foretold by Jeremiah.

This new kingdom is one in which as Christians, we have all been 'born'. Through our baptism we are citizens of this wonderful kingdom. Sometimes, however, we forget that this kingdom is not just something that will happen in the future. In some amazing way it is also partly here now. God's kingdom is both here in the present, and yet is also to come more fully in the future.

□ *Starter*

Create groups to look at a *just* kingdom. In the week before choose leaders and prime them as to their task. Allow the congregation to choose the group they wish to join, and offer at least one group suitable for young children (e.g. groups of 3 or 4 possibly):

Group 1   Discuss the following question: 'Men and women have been given free will. Is it possible for there to be a just society when everyone has the freedom to choose how they will live and behave?' How might this just society occur? Can you list some of the changes that need to be made? What changes can be made in your community now? List these on a large sheet of paper for all to see.

Group 2   Discuss the following question: 'What things need changing if God's kingdom is to hold sway in our world?' You might want to look at the national and international news in recent newspapers. List the changes that you would want to see. What changes can be made in your community now? List your conclusions on a large sheet of paper.

Group 3   Paint a large frieze. Half of the frieze should show the present world, and half show the world when God's kingdom is fully here. (For example: today's world might have chimneys belching out smoke, while God's world might be more environmentally friendly.) Make sure the group discuss the project before painting begins so that the two 'worlds' look distinctly different. It would probably be better to ask one person to quickly draw large shapes onto the frieze before everyone begins to paint. Provide old shirts for people to cover up their clothes, and put down paper or plastic to catch drips.

Group 4   Make crowns and talk about 'The Good King'. What is so different about the Good King? Look at Jesus as the Good King, and Herod as a bad king.

Group 5   Explore the notion of citizenship. What does it mean to be a citizen? What rights and privileges do citizens have? How easy or how hard is it to become a citizen of a land? What duties do citizens have? Listen to the experiences of any who have become citizens of a different country from where they were born. Then equate the conversation to God's kingdom. List the rights, privileges, and duties of a citizen in God's kingdom. Put these up onto a large sheet of paper for all to see.

☐   *Conclusion*

Gather the work of the groups together and hear back from each leader. What have the congregation learned about God's kingdom? Hang up all the work.

THE SECOND SUNDAY OF ADVENT

God the King is coming to judge his people; to sift them and weigh them. Will they be found worthy of his trust, and is there hope for our future?

Baruch 5.1–9 or Malachi 3.1–4
Philippians 1.3–11
Luke 3.1–6

- Old-fashioned scales.
- Felt-tip pen.
- Adhesive labels to mark + and − signs.
- Large number of small pieces of paper.
- Pencils for everyone.

□ *Starter*

Obtain a pair of old-fashioned scales, where one side balances against the other. Mark one end of the scale with a + sign, and one end with a – sign.

Give each member of the congregation a *small* piece of paper and a pencil. Encourage young children to draw rather than write, or to work with adults. Ask the congregation to identify *either* one good thing that a human being has done for the world or its people (e.g. drained the fens, or found a cure for smallpox), *or* one negative thing that a human being has done to the world or its people (e.g. poisoned rivers and seas, or engaged in continual warfare). It is not necessary to name an actual person.

When everyone has completed the task, ask them to come and place their piece of paper on one end of the scales, either on the positive (+) side or the negative (–) side, as appropriate. Inevitably there will probably be more pieces of paper on the negative side, and when the last person has come forward allow the scales to find their true position.

Discuss why the result occurred. Was everyone unduly pessimistic? Couldn't they think of positive examples? Why should this be so? Had they expected the result that was achieved?

□ *Comment*

The words from Malachi have a great sense of urgency about them. God is sending his messenger before him. Just as kings were in the habit of sending people to clear the way and make preparation for them, so he is sending someone to prepare his people. Out of the blue, says Malachi, the king our God will appear. He will appear when we are least expecting him.

But lest we think that this visit will be a time of rejoicing, he warns us that we are mistaken. The king will come to test us, and his coming will not be pleasant. For he comes to see of what we are made, to search out our impurities and our uncleanliness. Like a fire that sifts the pure from the impure, and a soap that removes the stain, God will sift and cleanse his people to leave only what is acceptable to him.

In St Luke's Gospel we see God's messenger, John, who is sent to preach a message of repentance to the people of Israel. God starts his work with the people of the covenant. They are to be prepared for the coming of the king who will weigh them in his scales, and judge them accordingly.

Comment that 'we have weighed the people of our world today' and found them wanting. We believe that humans have done more harm to the world and its people, than good. But is this is a true picture?

☐ *Note*

If the opposite conclusion was found, amend the last paragraph.

☐ *Conclusion*

Give out extremely small pieces of paper, all the same size, and ask the congregation to write down all the good things they have done in their life. For example: looked after Mum when she was poorly; did the shopping for a neighbour, etc. Now put down all the bad things. Each comment is to go on a separate sheet of paper. The pieces of paper should be folded so that the comments are unseen, and should of course be anonymous.

Remove the original pieces of paper from the scales, then collect in the new offerings and weigh them. Which side is the heaviest this time? Has there been any change at all? Is there cause for hope?

Finally, ask whether the situation could be changed? Can the congregation change their lives to create a difference? Allow a moment or two of silence for everyone to identify one or two changes that could be made. Invite everyone to come out and take *one* sheet from the negative side of the scales and transfer it to the positive side. The piece of paper does not need to be their own. Does the balance change significantly now?

THE THIRD SUNDAY OF ADVENT

We need to be ready to receive the king now, for the time of preparation is almost over.

Zephaniah 3.14–20
Philippians 4.4–7
Luke 3.7–18

- Large sheets of plain paper, or frieze paper.
- 3 parcels for 'Pass the parcel' with texts inside each layer.
- Music to accompany 'Pass the parcel'.
- Questions.
- OHP or flip-chart.
- Sheet of A5 paper for each group.
- Felt-tip pens for each group.

☐ *Starter*

Before the service put up large sheets of paper, or a length of frieze paper. If nowhere can be found for the paper, lay it along the floor in a suitable place. Also create two, three or four 'parcels' to be used in a game of 'Pass the parcel'. Each parcel needs as many layers as possible, and there should be sufficient parcels to allow every second or third person a chance of opening it. Inside each layer place one of the following texts from Zephaniah or from Luke. These should be muddled so that they do not come out in any particular order.

> 'Sing aloud, O daughter Zion' (Zephaniah 3.14a)
>
> 'shout, O Israel!' (Zephaniah 3.14a)
>
> 'Rejoice and exult with all your heart, O daughter Jerusalem!' (Zephaniah 3.14b)
>
> 'The Lord has taken away the judgements against you' (Zephaniah 3.15a)
>
> 'he has turned away your enemies' (Zephaniah 3.15b)
>
> 'The King of Israel, the Lord, is in your midst' (Zephaniah 3.15b)
>
> 'you shall fear disaster no more' (Zephaniah 3.15b)
>
> 'Do not fear, O Zion' (Zephaniah 3.16b)
>
> 'Do not let your hands grow weak' (Zephaniah 3.16b)
>
> 'The Lord, your God, is in your midst, a warrior who gives victory' (Zephaniah 3.17a)
>
> 'he will rejoice over you with gladness' (Zephaniah 3.17b)
>
> 'he will renew you in his love' (Zephaniah 3.17b)
>
> 'he will exult over you with loud singing as on a day of festival' (Zephaniah 3.17b)
>
> 'I will remove disaster from you, so that you will not bear reproach for it' (Zephaniah 3.18b)
>
> 'I will deal with all your oppressors at that time' (Zephaniah 3.19a)
>
> 'And I will save the lame and gather the outcast' (Zephaniah 3.19b)
>
> 'and I will change their shame into praise and renown in all the earth' (Zephaniah 3.19b)
>
> 'At that time I will bring you home, at the time when I gather you' (Zephaniah 3.20a)
>
> 'for I will make you renowned and praised among all the peoples of the earth when I restore your fortunes before your eyes, says the Lord' (Zephaniah 3.20b)
>
> 'You brood of vipers! Who warned you to flee from the wrath to come?' (Luke 3.7b)
>
> 'Bear fruits worthy of repentance' (Luke 3.8a)
>
> 'Do not begin to say to yourselves, 'We have Abraham as our

ancestor'; for I tell you, God is able from these stones to raise
up children to Abraham' (Luke 3.8b)

'Even now the axe is lying at the root of the trees' (Luke 3.9a)

'every tree therefore that does not bear good fruit is cut down
and thrown into the fire' (Luke 3.9b)

'Whoever has two coats must share with anyone who has none;
and whoever has food must do likewise' (Luke 3.11b)

'I baptize you with water; but one who is more powerful than I is
coming; I am not worthy to untie the thong of his sandals. He
will baptize you with the Holy Spirit and fire' (Luke 3.16)

'His winnowing-fork is in his hand, to clear his threshing-floor
and to gather the wheat into his granary; but the chaff he will
burn with unquenchable fire' (Luke 3.17)

Play a traditional game of 'Pass the parcel', but with three parcels.
Circulate the parcels around the congregation while music is
played. When the music stops the person holding the parcel should
open it and take out the quotation. Play the game as fast as
possible, and try to ensure that everyone finally has sight of one of
the quotations. Keep some duplicate quotations spare to cover any
that get lost in the unwrapping.

Invite the congregation to gather in small groups around those
with the quotations. Put up the following questions on an OHP or
flip-chart, and invite the congregation to ask themselves:

- To whom is the speaker talking?
- What does the quotation mean?
- What is the *emotional* tone of the text? Does the speaker seem
  happy, angry, etc? Is there a sense of urgency, or is the
  speaker relaxed and laid-back?
- What do you think a listener might feel when hearing this
  message?
- What does this text say for me today?

Children should work together with parents, and the questions can
be changed to suit them.

☐   *Conclusion*

While the groups are discussing the questions give out felt-tip pens
and pieces of A5 or smaller sized paper. Now direct each group to
write something very short in answer to the last question: 'What
does this text say for me today?'

Finally, encourage the groups to go and place the text and their
comment onto the large sheet of frieze paper. Allow time for
everyone to read all the comments.

7

□   *Comment*

After the warning of the dreadful cataclysm to come when the whole world will be consumed in God's burning anger and the very order of creation itself will be overturned, Zephaniah now gives us a passage of great hope as he looks even further into the future. The people are to 'rejoice and exult' with all their heart. The prophet looks beyond the time of anger to a time of great joy. They are to 'shout' a victory cry, like the cry they shouted in battle.

What is the reason for this great jubilation? The answer is quite simple; God has finished their time of punishment, he has also turned back their enemies, and he stands in the midst of them as their king. All of this calls for great celebration, for never again will they fear that evil will overwhelm them; never again will the lame or outcast be abandoned. God is in the midst of them.

In contrast Luke reminds us of the time of judgement that will come before Zephaniah's utopian world-order is in place. Here the sense of urgency is obvious. 'Even now the axe is lying at the root of the trees,' he says. God is coming to judge his people the Jews, and it is no good their claiming that they are followers of Abraham, for it will not stand them in good stead. The bad fruit is to be cut down and thrown into the fire. Only the good fruit is to be kept.

Besides this the ultimate Judge is already at work. The image of the 'winnowing-fork' already clearing the threshing floor on which he will sift the wheat is a powerful image. There is no longer any time to make reparation for a life mis-spent. It should have been accomplished already.

The warning is just as urgent today. God stands ready to judge us, his winnowing-fork in his hand. Our time of preparation for his coming again at Christmas is almost over. We need to be ready to receive him now, for he comes to judge the earth.

THE FOURTH SUNDAY OF ADVENT

God's plan for his world involves the willing acceptance of Zechariah and Elizabeth, and of Mary and Joseph of their roles, as told them by the angel. This week gives an opportunity to explore what we know about God's heavenly messengers.

Micah 5.2–5a
Hebrews 10.5–10
Luke 1.39–45 (46–55)

- Angel worksheets for all groups.
- Pencils or pens.
- Bibles.
- Texts.
- OHP or flip-chart.
- Fat felt-tip pens.
- Optional: Craft materials, angel templates, tables.

□ *Comment*

All of us are familiar with the notion of angels. We are accustomed
to seeing young children playing the parts of angels in the local
nativity play. We hang symbolic angels on our Christmas tree, and
we send Christmas cards with choirs of angels pictured on them!
But we must not forget that angels come from God, and in our
Bible they always bring important messages to men and women.

In our Gospel reading today we heard the middle part of a much
longer story about Zechariah, Elizabeth, Mary, Joseph and their
two babies. Zechariah is a God-fearing man, a priest, married to
Elizabeth and they have no children. While on duty in the Temple
an angel of the Lord appears to him promising he will have a
special child. He is to name the child John. Unfortunately
Zechariah doesn't believe the angel and is struck dumb, until the
prophecy comes true.

Sometime later another angel visits his wife's cousin, Mary. This
time it is the Archangel Gabriel who comes to foretell the birth of
Jesus. Mary understandably is afraid, but unlike Zechariah she
answers 'let it be with me according to your word' (Luke 1.38), and
accepts God's plans for her future.

These two incidents, though, are not the only times that God
sends his messengers to his people. In our Bible there are many
more such occurrences, and each can teach us something about
these special visitors as we shall see.

□ *Starter*

Before the service create an A4 sheet on the lines of that on page 10.
Divide the congregation into small mixed-age groups and give each
group an Angel worksheet, a pen or pencil, and as many Bibles as
possible. Instruct them to look up the texts in the Bibles and find
out all they can about the angels mentioned.

Genesis 16 v 5 – 14
Genesis 19 v 1 – 23
Genesis 31 v 11 – 13
Exodus 23 v 20 – 24

Numbers 22 v 22 – 35
Judges 13 v 2 – 23
2 Samuel 24 v 15 – 17

1 Kings 19 v 1 – 9
1 Chronicles 21 v 12 – 30
Daniel 3 v 12 – 30
Daniel 6 v 16 – 23

Matthew 1 v 18 – 25
Matthew 2 v 13 – 15
Matthew 4 v 11

Matthew 28 v 1 – 8
Luke 1 v 5 – 23
Luke 1 v 26 – 38
Luke 2 v 8 – 15

John 20 v 11 – 14
Acts 10 v 1 – 8
Acts 12 v 6 – 11

□ *Artwork*

Create a sheet decorated with angels. There should be space for people to fill in answers to the questions. The questions and answers could be in boxes or circles around the page or on the angels themselves. At the top of the page put: 'Find out about angels'. The texts could be put into a border all round the worksheet.

Questions

Does the angel have a name?
Who sends the angel?
Is there any mention of how they arrive?
Does the angel speak?
Is the angel seen by more than one person?
Note anything else of interest.

Texts

Genesis 16.5–14
Genesis 19.1–23
Genesis 31.11–13
Exodus 23.20–24
Numbers 22.22–35
Judges 13.2–23
2 Samuel 24.15–17
1 Kings 19.1–9
1 Chronicles 21.12–30
Daniel 3.12–30
Daniel 6.16–23
Matthew 1.18–25
Matthew 2.13–15
Matthew 4.11
Matthew 28.1–8
Luke 1.5–23
Luke 1.26–38
Luke 2.8–15
John 20.11–14
Acts 10.1–8
Acts 12.6–11

Ensure that anyone who would like to take home a spare worksheet has a copy.

□ *Conclusion*

Gather together the information discovered on an OHP or flip-chart. Are there similarities between the answers? Can general principles be established about the characteristics of these heavenly messengers?

□ *Optional*

Offer one or more craft groups for children or adults who might wish to explore the subject in a different way. For example: Create angels to hang on a Christmas tree, or above the crib in church.

CHRISTMAS DAY

Mary and Joseph travel to Bethlehem from Nazareth to register for the census imposed by a foreign emperor. While there Mary gives birth to her child, Jesus.

Isaiah 9.2–7
Titus 2.11–14
Luke 2.1–14 (15–20)

- Role-play leader.
- 4 or 5 actors.
- Costumes.
- Paper scrolls.
- Primed group of people.
- A–Z A4 sheets and Prit-tak or drawing pins.
- Optional: Map of the country and map pins.

□ *Starter*

Before the service place A4 landscape sheets, lettered A to Z, around the church. On each sheet put:

Name   Town of origin   Present town   Length of time to walk

Also before the service gather material to create costumes for a piece of role-play or drama. You will need the following adult characters:

- Emperor Augustus (someone suitably authoritarian).
- Local governor.
- 2 or 3 Roman soldiers.

Now create your own piece of drama or role-play based on the census collected in Palestine at the time of Jesus' birth. All of the actors will need some briefing or a rehearsal. Instruct them to provide all the bowing, servility, saluting, or authoritarian stance needed for their parts.

The task for the emperor is to order a census to be taken of all the people in his lands. Messengers are sent (bearing paper scrolls) to all parts of the world. One is received by the local governor in X (the country in which you live), who then orders his men to see that a census is carried out in the area under his jurisdiction.

Up until this point only the 'actors' have been involved. However, at this point the congregation become involved. The messengers and soldiers sent by the local governor now go to the congregation. Their instructions are to make sure that all the congregation register at their home town (that is the nearest town to where they were born). They unroll the scrolls and read the order to the people: e.g. 'The Emperor Augustus decrees that each person in his empire should go to their home town to be registered.'

The messengers and soldiers should then approach a suitably primed group of people and forcibly instruct them to register at their home (or birth) town, in order that the rest of the congregation can see what they too will have to do shortly. For example, the conversation might go like this:

Soldier   Where were you born then, Madam?

Woman   Blackpool, if it's all the same to you!

Soldier   Now, now, Madam! There's no need to be rude! I'm only doing my duty! You need to go back to Blackpool to register – over there – do you see the letter B? Just fill in your name, your home town, and where you've come from.

Woman   But that's over X miles away. It'll take me X days to walk that far!

Soldier   Nevertheless the emperor says you've got to register. So off you go! And don't forget to put down how many miles you've walked! *(to himself)* That'll give her something more to moan about!
(The soldier ensures that the next one or two people also go to their appropriate home towns.)

The soldiers continue to ensure that everyone in the congregation goes to register themselves. If there are questions about 'going as a family' rather than as individuals, then allow this to happen. Families can choose the father's or mother's home town! Anyone who doesn't know their birth town can go to the capital city of the country in which they live.

 ☐   *Note*
Information on distances will have to be guessed.

□ *Optional*

As the home towns are identified take the information and mark them onto a large map of the country (or world) with map pins.

□ *Conclusion*

Hold a plenary session to discuss the feelings the congregation had when ordered to travel to their home town. For example:

> - How long would it take to walk from their present home to their town of origin? (Who had the furthest, and who the nearest?)
> - How would the elderly or very young have felt?
> - What would it be like to walk this distance if you were nearly nine months pregnant (even riding a donkey would have been not much better than walking!)?
> - How would it have felt to leave your work – your farm, your factory, your school – behind?
> - What would it have been like to travel through occupied territory, always watched by the enemy's soldiers?
> - How would you have carried your food, and what food would you have taken?
> - Where would you have slept *en route* – the ground, a bed, an inn, in the fields?

□ *Comment*

Isaiah foretells the coming of Jesus as a human child, born of a human mother. But though born as a baby he is to be special. Isaiah says that this child is 'born for us, a son given to us' (Isaiah 9.6), and that all authority and power are to rest on him. He is to be the 'Wonderful Counsellor, Mighty God, Everlasting Father, Prince of Peace' (Isaiah 9.6b).

When we read this well-known passage we can forget the reality of the situation that occurred 2,000 years ago. A man and a very young woman became engaged to be married. This engagement was binding, but before they were married Joseph found that Mary was pregnant. He could have had her stoned to death, since the child was not his. But after a visit by an angel who told him that Mary had conceived the baby by the Holy Spirit, Joseph chose to obey God and marry her.

The story we have heard today in our Gospel reading is of Mary about to give birth. The emperor has decreed that she and her husband are to travel to the home town of his tribe – the house of David, at Bethlehem. This means a journey of days over rocky terrain, at the mercy of bandits, and with excess heat and lack of water to contend with – all this as Mary nears the time to give birth to her child.

We forget the realities of the story (of the heat, the tiredness, the worry of leaving the carpentry business, the enormous numbers of those who were travelling at this time) because we have created a rosy glow in our minds around the story. But it was a very hard journey for any human being, let alone for the king of the world and his mother to endure.

Today we have reminded ourselves of what it might be like for us if we were called to travel in such a way, and perhaps it has given us an insight into what the journey might have been like for Mary and for Joseph. We need to remember, though, that for them it was just the first part of an even longer journey. The next journey was to be harder still.

THE FIRST SUNDAY OF CHRISTMAS

Exploring the lives of the young Samuel and the young Jesus encourages us to think about the lessons we have learnt in our own lives.

1 Samuel 2.18–20, 26
Colossians 3.12–17
Luke 2.41–52

- 4 adults or children to speak on 'How I learnt a lesson!'

□ *Starter*
Before the service prime four adults or children to speak for a minute or two on the following subject: 'How I learnt a lesson!' Make sure that each person offers a different *way* of learning the lesson. For example: A lesson was learnt because they made a mistake; or because another person taught them; or because they were determined not to follow someone else's example. The lessons learnt can be humorous or serious, but all should be short.

□ *Comment*

In the Old Testament reading we see Samuel as a young boy. Given back to God by a grateful Hannah, because she had been unable to have children, he is growing up under the careful eye of Eli the priest at Shiloh. His mother has dedicated him as a Nazarite to the Lord. This is no limited dedication. She has given him to God for the whole of his lifetime, and during that time he will not drink strong drink, or cut his hair. So Samuel grows up under the direction of the elderly priest Eli at the temple, alongside Eli's own sons whom we are told are 'scoundrels'.

In the Gospel reading we see another young boy, the 12-year-old Jesus during a visit to the Temple in Jerusalem. This was probably at the time of his Bar Mitzvah, indicating that he has become a man according to Jewish Law, though we are told that after this visit he returned home and obeyed his parents.

Both Samuel and Jesus are carefully nurtured in the faith, though both would have been subject to the normal temptations of any growing boy. In Samuel's case he was close to Eli's sons who undoubtedly set him a bad example, and in Jesus' case he would have been tempted by peer pressure from other lads in the small provincial town of Nazareth. However, we are told that both found favour with God and with people: 'with divine and with human favour'. As they grew and matured they gradually learnt what it was God wanted of them, and what was to be their future life – one as a great prophet, and the other as the Messiah sent to save his people.

□ *Conclusion*

Invite the congregation to turn to their neighbour and tell them of one thing they learnt as a child (or young child in the case of children). After listening to each other's 'lesson' from the past, recount one learnt recently. Should some adults find it difficult to find a 'recent lesson' gently point out this might say something about their attitude to life, since we should all go on learning until our death!

□ *Optional*

Tell each other about 'the greatest lesson of my life'.

Finally spend a few moments in silence thinking about what has been learnt this day, and thanking God for the lesson.

THE SECOND SUNDAY OF CHRISTMAS

The start of the New Year brings an opportunity to create a Hopes List for the world.

Ecclesiasticus 24.1–12
Ephesians 1.3–14
John 1.(1–9) 10–18

- Paper and pencils.
- OHP or flip-chart and 3 transparencies or large sheets of paper.
- Fat felt-tip pen.
- 2 'tellers'.

☐ *Comment*

St John's Gospel begins in the nature of an epic film. It portrays the life of Christ before the world began – a life lived in union with God. He was not *created*, he existed for all time. St John uses the phrase 'the Word', which has already been used in the Old Testament. Here though, 'the Word of God' had a life of its own. It was conceived as a Person (see Psalm 33.6). And the Word, he says, 'was God' (John 1.1).

As if this were not enough the Word, through whom the world was created, became flesh. He became a man, living the life of those he had created. But the people to whom he came, God's people, the Israelites, rejected him. They did not know him, and they turned from him. The tragedy is that, except for a few men and women, the Jews rejected and disowned the very one for whom they had waited so long.

Those who believed then as well as those who believe now, whatever their race, have been given the greatest gift of all. They have the *right* to become the children of God. As Christians we become God's children from the time we accept him into our lives; but we also grow more like him as we get to know him. God is love, and as we come closer to him, we are transformed. We might like to think of God as leaving the mark of his presence on us! This is our great hope – a hope that should help us to transform the world around us.

□ *Starter*

Either in small mixed-age groups, or as a whole congregation, create 'Hopes for the World'. Adults should work with children. Initially keep the hopes global. What is it that the congregation would like to see changed in the world during the year? For example: That a certain war might cease; or that famine in Africa might be eradicated. No matter how idealistic the hopes, take any suggestions and write them up on an OHP or flip-chart.

Now complete the same task, on another sheet of transparency or flip-chart paper, for your own country. What is it that people would like to see changed this year? Finally, complete a third Hopes list for your own locality.

□ *Conclusion*

Many of the hopes may have been totally impracticable (however, remind the congregation that the end of apartheid and the Berlin Wall were considered impracticable wishes at one time), so now comes the task of paring them down. Encourage the congregation to work together in twos, and give each pair three small pieces of paper and a pencil. Their task is to choose one Hope from each of the three lists, and write it down on a separate piece of paper.

Collect the pieces of paper and count up the results. (This could be done by two people during a hymn if desired.) Point out that the hopes which come at the top of the three lists are those the congregation will continue to pray for, *and* hopefully work for, during the coming year. Finally, remind the congregation that as children of God, they should continue to take God's transforming love into every part of their world.

□ *Optional*

Discuss the Hopes list at the PCC or church council. Can the church as a body help any of these causes? Review in a year's time!

THE EPIPHANY

A study of the word 'Epiphany' and of the readings for the day teaches us more about this important festival.

Isaiah 60.1–6
Ephesians 3.1–12
Matthew 2.1–12

- Bibles.
- Dictionaries.
- Books on the Bible, on Isaiah, on Matthew and Luke, and on church festivals and customs.
- Large sheets of paper and fat felt-tip pens.

□ *Optional*

Before the service, or at some point in the service, play a tape or CD of 'O thou that tellest good tidings' (chorus, not the air) from Handel's *Messiah*. Afterwards point out that these words come from today's Old Testament reading (Isaiah 60.1). He is prophesying the glory that will come.

□ *Starter*

In the week before the service ensure that a number of workshop leaders are appointed, and offer as many workshops as possible. There can be duplicate workshops. All are designed to find out more about the Epiphany. The success of this work will depend upon the number of reference books and materials that can be provided, to allow the congregation a good quality of information. Put up titles for the workshops to help the congregation choose which they want to join.

Inform the congregation that today they are to learn all they can about the Epiphany. Invite them to join one of the groups.

□ *Workshops*

1 What's in a name?

Provide a number of very good dictionaries. Also provide a number of books that will give a theological insight into the meaning of the word 'Epiphany'. The task of the group is to find out what 'Epiphany' means. Notice there are at least three meanings. Allow everyone to look up the word 'Epiphany' before coming back together to discuss their findings. Then as a group look up the three readings for the day, and discuss how the word 'Epiphany' fits them. In other words, why have these readings been chosen?

2 The festival
Provide as many books as possible, or information from the web, on the festival of the Epiphany. The task of the group is to find out how the festival is celebrated across the world, and what significance it has for churches. What traditions are associated with the festival? Read Matthew 2.1–12 and look at the birth reading in Luke 2.1–20. Discuss the differences between Matthew and Luke. Does the group think the Matthew reading is myth or reality?

3 Symbol of light
Explore the imagery of light in today's Old Testament and Gospel readings. What does it mean, and why is it used? You may need to find out about Isaiah, and when Isaiah 60 might have been written. How does 'light' apply to Israel at this time? Look at the story of the star in Matthew's story. What is the modern thinking about this special star? Find out the meanings of the word 'Epiphany'; does light apply especially to these? How does light apply to the three Wise Men, who are not Jewish and who come from the east?

4 Isaiah's prophecy
Look at Isaiah 60.1–6. Using as many books on Isaiah as can be gathered, find out all you can about Isaiah – where did he live, at what time, etc. Decide whether you think there were one or three such prophets. Why is Isaiah 60 deemed to be so different from the

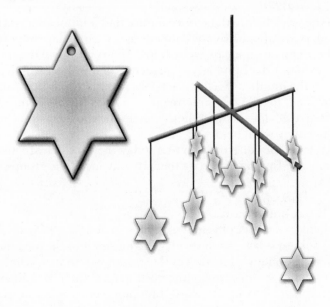

rest? Then begin to look at the meaning of Isaiah 60.1–6. As a group can you make sense of the words and apply them to the time in which they might have been written? Finally, decide how you think they apply to the festival of the Epiphany.

5 The Wise Men

Gather children under the age of 11 years together and tell them the story of the Fourth Wise Man (by Mig Holder, Coverdale). They might like to make star mobiles out of silver or gold tin foil, canes and string. On each star put the name of one person who has taught them about Jesus, or has read them Bible stories. The names may need to be stuck on, as it will be difficult to write on tin foil.

☐ *Comment*

In many churches today the festival of the Epiphany has been rather lost. The Wise Men have 'visited' the stable in the weeks before Christmas in many schools, and in most churches they have been sung about over the Christmas period. So when we get to January 6th it feels a little as though we have done this before – rather like eating the cold Christmas meats well into January. Not only this, but we think of January 6th as 'Twelfth Night' (with all its pagan significance) as well as the day when we remove all our Christmas decorations, so making it really feel like the end of Christmas.

But it is important that we separate the coming of the Wise Men from the stable scene, and give this festival its due significance. Until this moment the coming of God's Son to Mary and Joseph in the stable at Bethlehem was a Jewish phenomenon. He was to be the Messiah, the one who was to save God's people. All of this had no relevance, and no significance for the rest of the world, until the Wise Men arrived.

The Wise Men signify that God is offering salvation to the whole world. They are themselves Gentiles (non-Jews) and will take the good news back to their own countries to begin the work of God's salvation.

☐ *Conclusion*

Allow each group to tell the rest of the congregation everything they have discovered. It is important that adequate time is given for this, so that all the information is shared among the whole congregation.

21

THE FIRST SUNDAY OF EPIPHANY

God calls us by name to a close, personal, relationship. As Christians we are called to make this same relationship with others.

Isaiah 43.1–7
Acts 8.14–17
Luke 3.15–17, 21–22

- Books about names.
- 'Information Desk' or Desks and 'Information' signs.
- Paper and pencils.
- Plain badges or sticky labels.
- Large sheets of paper or frieze paper.
- Prit-tak or drawing pins.

☐ *Starter*

Collect together as many books about names as possible. You may find that young families have bought books when thinking of names for their children. If you can only find two or three such books, then set up an 'Information Desk(s)'.

Give everyone in the congregation a piece of paper and a pencil. Invite them to gather in mixed-age groups and to explore the meaning of their Christian name(s). It would be good if the congregation could be divided in such a way that each group contains someone whose name is not necessarily known to everyone. This could be achieved by asking people to go to a group represented by the first letter of their Christian name, e.g. Adam goes to Group A. If any group is too big, create another of the same letter; and if any groups are very small, combine them. Identify one 'runner' for every one or two groups (these could be children, or adults who have been helping to conduct the service, e.g. ministers, organist, readers, etc).

Each person is now to tell their group their Christian name (or names). The group should then try to guess what the name means. If the owner of the Christian name knows what it means they should then tell the group. When a name is unknown, the group should send a runner to the Information Desk for help. Where the meaning of a first name still cannot be found, proceed to look at a person's second name if possible.

When the meaning of all the names has been discovered, write the name and its meaning onto a small piece of paper. Finally, everyone should also write their Christian name(s) onto a badge and wear it. The badge could be something as simple as a sticky label.

☐ *Conclusion*

Before the service put up a number of large sheets of paper, or some frieze paper around the church, headed 'Called by Name'. Put a quantity of Prit-tak or drawing pins nearby, and invite everyone to come out and pin their name (on the small sheet of paper) up onto the large sheet of paper or frieze paper.

Finally invite everyone to spend some time greeting one another. They are to ask the same question of everyone they meet: 'What is your name and its meaning?' It is important to ask 'What is your name and its meaning?' of everyone, to help those with bad memories as well as those who are new. Allow plenty of time for the congregation to find out as many names and meanings as possible.

☐ *Comment*

Isaiah reminds the people that they have no reason to doubt God. They may have been taken off into exile, but God has not abandoned them. After all, God created them. He spoke the Word and like the earth and heavens before them, they were created. Next he formed them, as he formed Adam before them, and as if that weren't enough, when they fell into sin he redeemed them.

More than all this, Isaiah says, God has called each person by name and they are his people. For Jews to know someone's name is to know them intimately, to know their personality, since ideally a person's name was a description of that person. God *knows* his people in this way. He calls them as beloved sons and daughters.

If that is how God called his people the Jews, how much more does he call us by name. At our baptism we are *named*, (e.g. 'Amanda, I baptize you in the name of . . .') before God. Indeed in many countries Christians are given a new, a *baptismal*, name, which is different from their given or birth name. This name is often a saint's name. Indeed some clergy are unhappy about baptizing people with names that are not known to be *Christian* names.

We were called by God and each one of us has responded to that call. He holds us close, as the closest, most beloved, children. He knows each one of us by name. But perhaps this should give us pause for thought, though. How many of us know each other by name? How important is it to overcome the problems of our memory and make a point of knowing other Christians by name, as the beloved of God? Knowing one another by name is the beginning of creating a close relationship with one another.

□ *Optional*
Encourage everyone to find ways of learning people's names, for example by associating the first letter with other things, e.g. Arty Amanda, Vera the Vole.

THE SECOND SUNDAY OF EPIPHANY

God gives the gifts of his Spirit for the good of the whole church community. We need to make sure they are used, and that we allow these gifts to mature and grow for the good of all.

Isaiah 62.1–5
1 Corinthians 12.1–11
John 2.1–11

- 4 or more speakers.
- Large sheets of paper already prepared, and some blank ones.
- Prit-tak or drawing pins.
- Pencils or fat felt-tip pens.

□ *Starter*
Invite at least four people to speak about the work that they do for the church, and in particular the 'gifts' (or abilities) that enable them to do this work. For example, the organist needs to have a natural ability to understand rhythm, and to be able physically to play a number of notes at the same time. After this comes years of practice, but all of this would be useless if there were no natural gift initially.

Keep the speakers to a short time-limit, and ensure they spend as much time looking at the gifts and abilities that have made them able to do the task for the church, as well as at the job itself.

□ *Comment*
In his first letter to the Corinthians St Paul is dealing with a church that seems to need some help. We don't know exactly what has gone wrong, but whatever it is Paul is concerned that the congregation realize the necessity for a united but diverse church.

This sounds impossible, but God, he says, has both unity and diversity. This is part of the character of God himself. God is one Lord, one Spirit, and one God. St Paul argues that in the same way the church too should celebrate unity in diversity. A healthy church should always celebrate its diversity.

The Spirit is given to the church. The different gifts given by the Spirit are always for the benefit of the church (that is, the building up of the body of Christ, not the church building!). To one is given the gift of faith, to another the gift of healing, and to another the gift of wisdom. None of these gifts of the Spirit are given for the individual's benefit, they are all given for the benefit of the church. St Paul says they are given 'for the common good'.

Throughout our lives the Spirit continues to give his gifts, so we may find ourselves doing different jobs over the years. The Christian life is always about *growing* in faith, not about standing still.

☐   *Conclusion*

Working in small groups (or by simply turning to a neighbour), invite the congregation to think about the work they do for the church. If there are visitors present, they might like to speak about the church they usually attend. Newcomers and children might like to think about what they could offer the church.

Before the service create headed sheets of paper and place around the church. Place each sheet at some distance from the others, if possible, and put a pencil or pen nearby. Each sheet should have a heading of one job that is done for the church, e.g. Churchyard Work; Choir; Sunday School; Cleaning; Leading Services; Bell-ringers, etc. It may well be that someone will identify a job not thought of by anyone else, so have some spare sheets available.

Invite everyone to leave their seat and put their name down against any job they do for the church. As people are beginning to finish the task put up a new blank sheet (or more than one) and invite the congregation to think about learning a new job (this may mean giving up an old one!). Cross their name off the old list and place it on the new list.

Be sure to follow up all suggestions afterwards. Some people will need training. Some may not have the gifts necessary for the task, and will need gently discouraging. But some may find a new lease of life.

THE THIRD SUNDAY OF EPIPHANY

St Paul speaks of the different parts of the church as limbs of one body, and of each limb as important to the body.

Nehemiah 8.1–3, 5–6, 8–10
1 Corinthians 12.12–31a
Luke 4.14–21

- Large sheets of paper.
- A4 sheets of card.
- Fat felt-tip pen.
- Some speakers.
- OHP or flip-chart.

□   *Starter*
If last week's suggestions were used, continue by looking at all the different jobs identified. Otherwise, start by putting up large sheets of paper around the church and identifying every job done for your church (for example: Intercessor, Cleaner, Bell-ringer, etc).

Before the service invite a number of people to talk about the work they do for the church. These speakers should be different from those used last week. This time they are to concentrate on *those on whom they rely to do their job*, and as they mention others, those people should be invited out (or their representatives) and given a placard showing their job. If the choir or some other large organization gets mentioned, all should come out to the front and be given one placard.

Be selective as to whom you ask to speak, and encourage them to think widely around their work, to identify everyone on whom they rely. It might be helpful to ask someone who works for the church but whom few appreciate.

□ *Optional*
The minister could try to enumerate all on whom he or she relies! This will most likely end in chaos, since almost everyone in the church will find themselves coming forward. It could be salutary, if the congregation does not appreciate each other's gifts and skills.

□ *Note*
Visitors, the elderly, the very young, and newcomers may all need reassurance. The elderly could be involved since many pray for others in the church; newcomers can be invited to help in the future; visitors can be asked about the tasks they do in their own church.

□ *Comment*
St Paul reminds us in the reading today that each person in the church is like a limb of the body. Just as we cannot manage without the heart or the head, so we cannot manage without each limb of the church. No part is greater than any other, though some may have prominence at one time over another. All parts are needed if the body of the church is to be healthy, and not become a monstrosity.

As we have seen we each depend upon one another for the smooth running of the church. For the conduct of worship, for the smooth running of a funeral or wedding, many people are involved. Each one is dependent on the other, so that their task is carried out smoothly and effectively. Indeed the church cannot be called a community if the work is done by only one person.

Comment on any inequalities that were discovered – perhaps where the church is relying too much on one person, or on one age-group. Keeping away from personalities, talk about the need for everyone to be involved for the church to be a healthy community.

□ *Conclusion*

Having looked at how the church works now look at its main work – evangelism. Remind the congregation this was the only instruction given to the disciples by Jesus after his resurrection. They were told to 'Go . . . and make disciples of all nations' (Matthew 28.19).

Start by giving a simple definition of 'evangelism'. For example: To communicate the gospel. Then explore how the gospel might be communicated. Take suggestions and put them up on an OHP or flip-chart. Encourage the congregation to think as widely as possible. Suggestions might include:

preaching in church
Bible study/Emmaus/Alpha groups
posters with slogans
use of parish magazine to speak about the gospel
gossiping the gospel with friends and neighbours
taking assemblies at local schools
opening the church for exhibitions
speaking at clubs about the work of the church

□ *Optional*

Draw up an *ideal* notion of who should be involved in this work, along the lines of the work done earlier, e.g. clergy, PCC or church management group, preachers, administrator, leaders of children's work, those with artistic talents, those with time to organize exhibitions or visit clubs, all church members. Take these conclusions to your church management group and continue the discussion and work.

THE FOURTH SUNDAY OF EPIPHANY

We are reminded that love always shows itself in some kind of action.

Ezekiel 43.27—44.4
1 Corinthians 13.1–13
Luke 2.22–40

- Group leaders.
- Copies of 1 Corinthians 13 for everyone.
- Newspapers and magazines.
- Glue.
- Scissors.
- Large sheets of card or sugar paper.
- Bible encyclopaedias.
- Bibles and/or copies of the New Testament.
- Paints.
- Frieze paper.
- Prit-tak or drawing pins.
- Acrylic paint, brushes, white candles, candle holders, and old shirts for overalls.

□ *Starter*

Before the service set up as many mixed-age groups as necessary for the size of the congregation, and appoint group leaders. The groups will each take one section of 1 Corinthians 13, to explore this remarkable statement about love. Choose any of the following tasks, or create others, as desired. If necessary have duplicate groups, and use adjacent rooms or buildings as well as the church, if available. Groups will need to have copies of the New Testament, or Bibles.

Group 1   Discuss the meaning of the word 'Love', in all its variations. Explore questions like: What does the world make of this word, today? What did St Paul mean by 'love' (or 'charity')? Do different generations understand the word to mean different things? Allow at least 5–7 minutes, depending on the time available, for discussion. Then give the group a large number of newspapers and magazines, and ask them to cut out articles that demonstrate the different meanings of love. These should then be pasted onto large sheets of card or sugar paper and put up in church.

Group 2   Using some Bible encyclopaedias, find out what the Corinthians were like. Why was it necessary for St Paul to write such a letter to them? What seems to have been wrong in their church? Allow five minutes for research, and then pool the information found. Take the first three verses of 1 Corinthians 13 and explore the meaning of these verses in the light of the information discovered. What is St Paul complaining about in the Corinthians' behaviour? What does the group think 'If I speak in the tongues of mortals and of angels' might mean? Can they guess the kind of person St Paul is speaking to in verses 2 and 3? Write up some large pithy headlines on sugar paper and card to indicate the problems at Corinth, e.g. 'The Corinthians were . . .' Put up in church for others to see.

Group 3   Explore the meaning of verses 4–6 in 1 Corinthians 13. Read them through and discuss their meaning. Then tell each other stories of people you have known with these loving characteristics. Mention any members of the congregation or community who fit these categories. Finally list some of the examples (e.g. 'Gardening for a neighbour who is ill') under a heading of 'Love is patient, love is kind . . .', and write up on a large sheet of paper using a fat felt-tip pen. Put up on the wall for others to see.

Group 4   Explore the notion of 'Love never ends' (1 Corinthians 13.8). Discuss the meaning of this statement as a group. Then find examples in the Bible where love endures and does not give up, using both the Old and New Testaments. Write these examples onto large sheets of paper, using a fat felt-tip pen, under a heading of 'Love never ends'.

Group 5   Discuss 'Love' in today's terms, and then as meant by St Paul. Our world believes it knows what 'love' is, would you agree? Look at 1 Corinthians 13, and allow at least 5–7 minutes for discussion on the passage and on the two different periods. Then take some large sheets of paper and a fat felt-tip pen. Write 'Love is' on the sheet, and invite members of the group to offer words or short phrases that seem appropriate.

Group 6   Discuss 'Love' in today's terms, and then as meant by St Paul in 1 Corinthians 13. Keep the discussion to concrete examples of love, and after a few moments offer the group paints and a large piece of frieze paper. Put up a heading of 'Love is', and allow the group to paint images conjured up by the discussion. When dry hang the frieze in church. The group should try to work together in a way that reflects the subject of love!

Group 7   Read 1 Corinthians 13.1–7. Discuss the meaning of love as used by St Paul. Then apply his thoughts to your church. Where is such love shown? How might it be better shown? (Keep the discussion away from personalities, and look at how the church as a whole can improve.) Take a large sheet of paper and a fat felt-tip pen. Put up a heading of 'Love in our church'. Underneath this draw a vertical line, and put a heading on the left of 'Well done', and a heading on the right of 'Could do better'. Examples of

'Well done' might be: visiting, or welcoming new people into church. Examples of 'Could do better' might be visiting nursing homes or working with young children. Put up the sheet for all to see.

Group 8   Explore the meaning of love with younger children. Make sure that each young child has one or two adults with them. One of the adults should not be a parent. The work with this group is to be a practical demonstration of love. Talk about whom they love, and who loves them. Mention that Jesus loves them, and that he died for them. Carry out a craft activity which involves helping one another. For example: Paint Christian symbols on white candles standing in candle holders, using acrylic paints and old shirts as overalls. Put down paper or plastic to stop splashes! Leave the candles to dry. The children can take the finished candles home and give them to people they love.

□   *Comment*

As some of the groups have discovered, the people of Corinth might speak in tongues, they might prophesy, and they might have amazing knowledge about their faith, but their lifestyle was appalling. They managed to have all the correct religious trappings, but somehow they had lost their love for one another. Their actions were all right, but their motives were all wrong. They were full of pride and arrogance, and cared about how they looked and sounded, but they had forgotten that what matters is *why* we do things.

For St Paul love is not just something abstract and spiritual. He's not a poet talking in an airy way about love. For him love is an *action*. If you possess love, says St Paul, you have to *act*. If you don't act, then you don't possess love. In his previous chapter in Corinthians he has been talking about the spiritual gifts – gifts like wisdom, faith, healing, miracles, prophecy, and the gift of tongues. Now, he says, love is the way in which these gifts function.

If you have the spiritual gift of faith, then it will be seen in the way you act towards another person, who may not have that faith. To have love means to act lovingly towards others, and to seek their good. In other words we should behave to others in the way God (in Christ) has behaved towards us. This is the kind of life all Christians are called to live, it is one of love in action.

□   *Conclusion*

Encourage everyone to look at each other's work. Alternatively ask leaders and group members to report back to the whole congregation on their discussions, or on what has been discovered or created.

PROPER 1

Sunday between 3 and 9 February inclusive (if earlier than the Second Sunday before Lent)

God's call always brings with it a task. What has God given us to do, and have we accomplished the task, or have we become side-tracked?

Isaiah 6.1–8 (9–13)
1 Corinthians 15.1–11
Luke 5.1–11

- My Time sheets for everyone
- Pencils.
- Information on PCC or church committee subjects.

□ *Starter*

Before the service create some small sheets headed 'My Time'. Divide the page into two columns, and number each column vertically from 1 to 10. Give out copies of the sheet and pencils to every member of the congregation. Young children should work with adults.

Ask the congregation to think about an average week, and to identify what they spend most of their free time doing (other than work, school, or sleep). 'No cheating please!' The most amount of time spent on any task will be number 1. For example, they might create a list like this:

My Time	
1 Watching television	1
2 Cooking	2
3 Cleaning	3
4 Ironing	4
5 Washing	5
6 Talking to the children	6
7 Walking the dog	7
8 Shopping	8
9 Emmaus group	9
10 Church	10

Invite everyone to turn to their neighbour and discuss the way they spend their time. What are their first reactions?

 □ *Comment*

All three readings today concentrate on God's call. In the Old Testament we see God calling Isaiah. In 1 Corinthians we read that St Paul was called, and in the Gospel reading we hear about the call of the first disciples.

There is one other thing these three readings have in common. In each case the person called is given a task to do. Isaiah is called to go as a messenger to the Israelites with a strange message which they will not understand. St Paul was called on his way down the Damascus road to take God's word to the Gentiles and to tell them that 'Christ died for our sins' (1 Corinthians 15.3b). Lastly, Jesus calls Simon, James and John to catch not fish, but men.

God does not call people without there being a task attached. So when we are called to become Christians there is always a task for us to do. We are called to a job.

We therefore need to ask ourselves, what has God called me to do as a Christian, and am I carrying out that task satisfactorily? A quick look at our list of priorities, of how we spend our week, might help us to see whether we are spending a suitable amount of time on the work God is calling us to do as Christians, and whether our priorities are right.

 □ *Conclusion*

Invite the congregation to return to the time sheets, and spend a few moments thinking about the way they are spending their time. Would they like to change the way their time is allocated? If so, ask them to rewrite the categories on the right. Keep the time allocation sensible, rather than too unrealistic.

Remind the congregation to go away and try to allocate their time as they would prefer, rather than as they now find exists.

PROPER 2

Sunday between 10 and 16 February inclusive (if earlier than the Second Sunday before Lent)

Without God we are spiritually impoverished; with God we are like a tree that receives water.

Jeremiah 17.5–10
1 Corinthians 15.12–20
Luke 6.17–26

- Copies of the Beatitudes for each group.
- Bibles.
- Information on saints.
- Flip-chart.
- Large sheets of sugar paper or card.
- Fat felt-tip pens.
- Prit-tak or drawing pins.
- Items representing the riches of the world, e.g. £ signs, pictures of cars, jewellery, etc.

☐ *Starter*

In the week before the service appoint group leaders, willing to do some preparation. During the service divide the congregation into groups of 6–8 people. These can be mixed-age groups, although children and teenagers may prefer to work together so the material can be adapted to their ages. All the groups will need copies of the Beatitudes: Luke 6.20–26.

Group 1 Look at Luke 6.20. As a group discuss the meaning of this sentence. Conclusions might be: This verse was spoken to disciples who had just been chosen, and who had given up everything to follow Jesus; the word 'poor' refers to both physical and spiritual poverty and the disciples had been made aware of their own spiritual poverty in relation to God's bounty.

Group 2 Look at Luke 6.21a. As a group discuss the meaning of this sentence. Conclusions might be: This verse does not refer to physical hunger, but to spiritual hunger; it is a desire to be forgiven and to receive mercy; it is a desire to be at one with God; it is a desire to be cleansed from all sin.

Group 3   Look at Luke 6.21b. As a group discuss the meaning of this sentence. Conclusions might be: This verse does not refer to those who mourn after someone dies, though it does conjure up the bitterness of such mourning; it refers to the grief that takes place in us because of our sin; it may refer to the grief that occurs for the sin of the whole world; such sin separates us from the love of God, and we can only mourn.

Group 4   Look at Luke 6.24. As a group discuss the meaning of this sentence. Conclusions might be: This denunciation is made to those who trust in earthly riches; it is not just aimed at those who are rich, but on those who care about attaining the things of this world; all of us behave like this occasionally.

□   *Conclusion*

Group 1   Before the service the leader should prepare some information on a number of saints or on Christians considered to be very holy. Make sure the information identifies their special characteristics (e.g. bravery, humility, perseverance, or faithfulness, etc.). Discuss the special characteristics shown by each person. In what way were they spiritually rich? Finally allow a moment's silence for each person to acknowledge in private in what way they might be spiritually *poor*.

Group 2   Give each member of the group a Bible. Ask individuals (or work in pairs) to find stories that give an example of those who are spiritually poor, but who desire to be at one with God. Alternatively identify some stories that show this characteristic (e.g. the Pharisee and the tax-collector, the thief on the cross, some psalms, the woman who washed Jesus' feet, etc.), and read them together. Close with prayer, or allow a time of silence for individuals to identify their own spiritual *hunger* (or lack of it) and ask God for help.

Group 3   Identify what is meant by 'sin', and then write up as many sins as possible onto a flip-chart or large sheet of paper. Try to list those sins many of us commit, rather than those that 'others' commit. Although murder may get a mention, it is more important that pride and greed are identified on the list. Finally, close with silence to allow each group member to identify their own besetting sins, and to offer them to God, in *sorrow*.

Group 4   Offer the group a selection of pictures that represent the riches of this world, e.g. pictures of cars, money or £ signs, houses, exotic holidays, private schools, beautiful lounges, jewellery, etc. Supply as many pictures of each item as possible, since the whole group may choose the same item. If there are other groups also looking at verse 24 then work together before the service to offer as many choices as possible. Finally, encourage the group to choose one item that they feel has undue emphasis in their own life, and has taken precedence over God. Allow time for silent prayer, before encouraging the members of the group to place the pictures of the items on the altar as recognition of their desire to change.

 ☐ *Comment*

In the Old Testament reading we heard Jeremiah say: 'Blessed are those who trust in the Lord, whose trust is the Lord.' The person who turns to God, who does not forsake him, is like a tree, planted near water whose roots are fed by the stream, so that even in a time of drought it will survive and its leaves will stay green. Jeremiah has known a time of drought in his own life. God seemed far away at that time. However, he recognizes that it was his own fault.

In the Gospel reading the same idea predominates. Without God we are spiritually impoverished. Only when we remain close to him and follow his ways are we to be blessed. Those who put their trust in the things of this world have chosen the wrong path, and are in a spiritual desert.

PROPER 3

Sunday between 17 and 23 February inclusive (if earlier than the Second Sunday before Lent)

The creation of a new set of Commandments helps to focus our minds on what Jesus meant by 'Love your neighbour as yourself'.

Genesis 45.3–11, 15
1 Corinthians 15.35–38, 42–50
Luke 6.27–38

- OHP or flip-chart.
- Fat felt-tip pen.
- Ten New Commandments list for everyone.
- Pencils.

□ *Starter*

Give out copies of the Ten Commandments (see Exodus 20.2–17), or put them up onto an OHP or flip-chart for all to see. Spend a moment or two looking at them, to refresh everyone's memory. Notice that the commandments are mostly negative, not positive.

Now invite everyone to create some new commandments. Keep them positive where possible. Write all suggestions onto an OHP or flip-chart, accept everything, and simply put them down in the order they are given. For example:

- Love your children.
- Give to the poor.
- Love God.
- Help those in distress.
- Love your parents.
- Care for the earth.

When the suggestions have dried up, begin to pare them down to *ten* new commandments with the help of the congregation. For instance: Can any of the suggestions be amalgamated? Are some deemed to be more important than others? Don't give in to the suggestion that 'If we love our neighbour we can ignore all the rest', at least at this stage. Emphasize that you are looking for *ten* commandments!

Finally when the task has been completed, put the new list into an order of priority. This may be difficult, but if possible make an attempt.

□ *Comment*

In our Old Testament reading we have seen that Joseph's treatment of his brothers is the opposite to what might be expected. Despite the dreadful thing they had done to him and to his father (in selling Joseph into slavery and convincing Jacob that he was dead), Joseph greets his brothers with open arms. He is to be their protector. He is to give them a home and provide food for them at this time of drought. The brothers must surely have been amazed at his generosity.

Jesus also picks up the same theme in the closing words of the Beatitudes. His words must have seemed startling to those who were

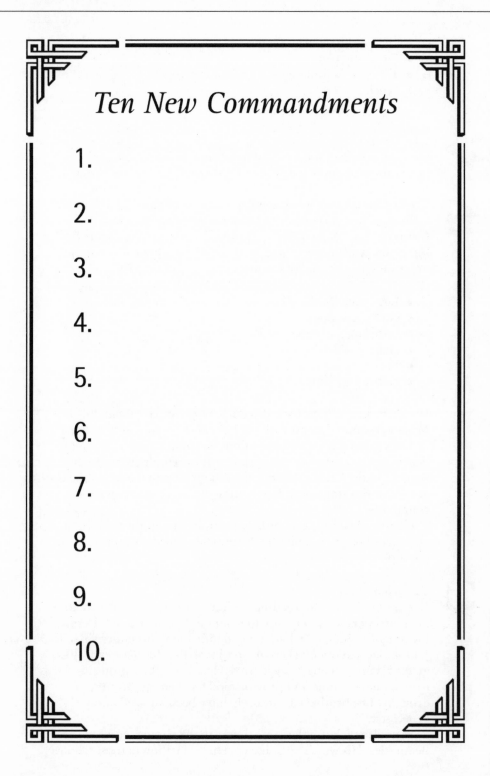

Ten New Commandments

1.

2.

3.

4.

5.

6.

7.

8.

9.

10.

listening. The Law of Moses taught that one should put love before vengeance, but the scribes and the Pharisees taught that this only applied to the 'children of Moses'. In other words it was all right to bear a grudge against a Gentile or an outsider. Yet here is Jesus saying that we should love everyone, and especially our enemies.

There was to be no element of choice. All people are to be our neighbours, and if they are in need, they are to be helped. God's love is to pass down to all people, whatever their circumstances. The crime itself might still be hated, but the criminal was to be shown God's love.

☐ *Conclusion*

Give each member of the congregation a blank Ten New Commandments list (see page 38). Give out pens or pencils, and ask everyone to copy down the finished list of Ten New Commandments. Children and adults should work together.

Encourage the congregation to take the list home and place it somewhere where it can be seen. If desired, put into the parish magazine, or 'tidy-up' the final version and make neat copies for everyone.

THE SECOND SUNDAY BEFORE LENT

We stretch our minds to cope with the unimaginable when we think of God. Nevertheless our response should be to offer him praise and worship, and we should spend our lives getting to know him better.

Genesis 2.4b–9, 15–25
Revelation 4
Luke 8.22–25

- Bibles for everyone (or to be shared between two people).
- OHP or flip-chart and fat felt-tip pen.
- List of psalms.
- Frieze paper.
- Paints.
- Tables or floor space.

□ *Starter*

Give out Bibles or copies of Revelation 4 to everyone, and encourage them to read through the description of God. They might also like to look at Isaiah 6.1–4 as well.

Invite everyone to turn to their neighbour and discuss this question: 'If you were asked to draw a picture of God what would he look like?' Allow a few minutes for discussion, and then ask for suggestions. Write up brief notes onto an OHP or flip-chart. For example:

old man
sunshine
abstract patterns
picture of Jesus
king on a throne

At this point if anyone wants to go and paint a picture of God encourage them to do so. Provide a large sheet of frieze paper and paints, either laid out on tables or on the floor. Put down plastic to protect the floor.

Continue working with the remainder of the congregation. What characteristics are the congregation keen to identify when 'drawing a picture' of God? List these characteristics. For example, some of these might be:

love
permanence
eternal
Creator
justice

□ *Conclusion*

Either working as a whole congregation or in small groups, look up as many psalms as possible and begin to identify texts that teach us something about the character of God.

Some psalms that teach us about God	
3.3	18.28
7.7–8	19.7
8.3–9	23.1–3
9.9	25.8
11.5	34.10
11.7	34.15
12.6	34.18
16.7	45.6
18.2	50.3–4
18.6	

Hold a plenary session if necessary to look at the artwork that has been done, and to hear from different groups.

☐ *Comment*

In the readings today we have seen God acting in different ways. In Genesis God creates the world, and in particular a man and a woman. (If desired, comment on the use of myth here.) God is the Creator of the whole world; there is nothing made that was not made without him. He is involved with all life, and with every aspect of our lives.

In the New Testament reading from Revelation we have a picture of God Almighty on a throne with all manner of beings before him, all offering praise, while in the Gospel reading we see Jesus, God as man, calming the storm.

Sometimes we forget that God appears in different ways to different people. He is Creator, judge, shepherd and pastor. He is there when we need comfort, and he is there when we need prompting to action. He is much more than we can ever conceive. Our response to him should simply be one of praise and adoration. Our desire should be to get to know him better.

THE SUNDAY NEXT BEFORE LENT

Our lives can be full of mountain-top experiences and down-in-the-valley experiences. Jesus also experienced the heights and the depths on earth, but it was his faith in God's presence in his life, as well as the fact that he was doing God's will, which sustained him.

Exodus 34.29–35
2 Corinthians 3.12—4.2
Luke 9.28–36 (37–43)

- Paper and pencils for everyone.
- Jigsaw pieces made out of card.
- Felt-tip pens for everyone.

□ *Starter*

Give each member of the congregation a small piece of paper and a pencil. Then ask them to identify a time in their life when they felt they were 'on a mountain-top', in other words when things were good and they felt marvellous. Turn to each other and share this.

Allow a moment or two for discussion and then call 'time'. Ask them to write down any words that come into their heads to describe how they felt at that moment. For example: ecstatic, happy, wonderful, great, etc.

Next invite them to think of a time when they have been 'down in the valley', when things have been bad, and they've felt as if the end of the world had come. If possible, share this with their neighbour.

Again allow a moment or two for everyone to talk. Call 'time' and again ask them to write down any words that describe how they felt. For example: devastated, unhappy, gutted, dreadful, etc. Put all these words down on the *reverse* side of the sheet of paper.

□ *Comment*

St Luke says that Jesus went up onto a mountain to pray, taking with him Peter, James and John. We are unsure which mountain they climbed, but wherever it was they found a place to be alone. While here Jesus experiences something which is to foreshadow his resurrection. St Luke says 'while he was praying the appearance of his face changed, and his clothes became dazzling white' (Luke 9.29). As well as this two men appear beside him. The disciples waking suddenly from sleep believe they are seeing Moses and Elijah.

We don't completely understand the meaning of this strange event. Perhaps it occurred to give Jesus the courage to face the coming days, and to give the disciples faith. The presence of Moses and Elijah would have led Jews to believe that the Law and the Prophets were in agreement with the path that Jesus was taking. But the voice of God himself is also heard giving his blessing to his Chosen One, and urging the disciples to 'listen to him!'

After this amazing 'mountain-top experience' the four men make their way down the mountain the next day to find a great crowd of people in the valley. Amid the noise and the shouting they are made aware there is a problem. The disciples have been unable to cure a lad who is seized with convulsions. The father is desperate, for it is his only son. But no matter what the disciples do, they cannot cure him. Their faith has not been sufficient.

From his mountain-top experience Jesus is suddenly thrust into a 'down-in-the-valley' experience. From the affirmation received from God he is plunged into the squabbling and lack-of-faith brawl at the foot of the mountain. For Jesus, it is his faith which sustains him. He knows he is treading the path that God wants.

□ *Conclusion*

Before the service create large jigsaw pieces out of card. The congregation will need two pieces of the jigsaw each. Each piece should fit onto an A4 sheet of paper.

Give out the jigsaw pieces and as many large felt-tip pens of any colour as you can possibly find (at least one between two). Invite the congregation to choose one word from their 'mountain-top' list and one word from the 'down-in-the-valley' list. On one piece write the one mountain-top word, and on the other piece write the down-in-the-valley word.

Finally create two jigsaws – one to represent the mountain-top experiences in their lives, and the other representing the down-in-the-valley experiences in their lives. Leave on the floor for all to look at later.

□ *Optional*

The jigsaw could be created at the end of the service.

ASH WEDNESDAY

Ash Wednesday is the day to look at ourselves, to explore what kind of person we really are, as opposed to the facade we often show to others.

Isaiah 58.1–12
2 Corinthians 5.20b—6.10
Matthew 6.1–6, 16–21

> - Masks for the role-play.
> - 3 actors for the role-play.
> - Mask cards for all the congregation, straws, scissors, sellotape.

☐ *Starter*
Create a short piece of role-play to demonstrate the kind of people we might be behind the 'mask' that is our face. Use three people: Angry Man, Proud Woman, and Jealous Child (see examples below). They should all be members of one family, and should hold a mask before their face. The following scenario would be suitable for the role-play, but another could be used:

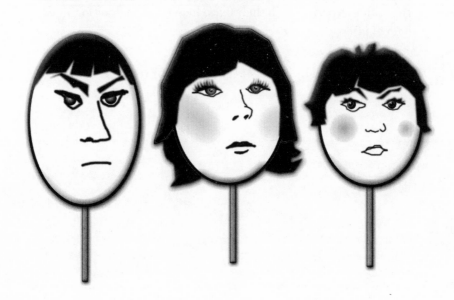

Role-play
Father returns home, not having got his expected promotion.
Someone else has been given the job, and he is very angry about
the situation. He takes it out on his wife and child. His wife is
only concerned with her standing in the community, and with
all that they possess. Her pride makes her unable to sympathize
with her husband. The whole conversation between the two
parents is punctuated by their daughter (or son) who is only
interested in the fact that her friend is going on a skiing holiday,
and has all the latest fashion clothing. She sees that what has
happened to her father will affect her chances of going skiing.

☐ *Comment*
In our Old Testament lesson today we see Isaiah complaining
about the people's attitude towards God and each other. They only
serve their own interests he says, when they fast. They do not
humble themselves before the Lord, and admit their sin. Neither are
they concerned for the poor or those who seek justice. Instead they
spend their time arguing and quarrelling with one another. In turn,
he says, God will not listen to their cries.

Matthew is equally dismissive of the way the people behave. He
reminds them not to make their piety obvious in order to show off,
or to give alms so that others see what they are doing, or to pray in
public places. All is to be done in secret so that only God knows
what they are doing.

Today we have been discovering the two sides of ourselves. To
the outside world we often present one face or 'mask', but behind
this usually lies another. We may appear kind and loving to the
outside world, but underneath there may be pride, jealousy, anger,
bitterness or envy. Our friends and neighbours may have no
knowledge of the real us, or may only occasionally glimpse this side
of us. The rest of the time we may hide behind our outward mask so
that our real self is unseen.

Ash Wednesday marks the start of the penitential season of Lent,
and is therefore a good day to begin to acknowledge the real self
that we keep hidden. It is also a good day to begin the work of
making ourselves more like the Lord whom we worship. But the
work of restoration must always begin with self-appraisal.

☐ *Conclusion*
Before the service photocopy the masks on page 44 on to A4 card,
or make your own, for every member of the congregation. The
masks should all represent aspects of ourselves that we prefer not to
acknowledge, for example, anger, jealousy, envy, gluttony or pride.

Give out the mask pictures, scissors, straws and sellotape. Get the congregation to cut out the masks, including the eye and mouth holes, and to attach the straws with sellotape.

Now invite everyone to turn to their neighbour, place the mask in front of their face and talk about the kinds of things that we don't show other people. For example: unkind thoughts, anger, greed, or pride. The conversations could be impersonal, e.g. looking at all the things people hide behind their faces, or it can be specific if people feel safe enough to talk about what they hide behind their own personal 'mask'. Children should work with adults, if possible.

THE FIRST SUNDAY OF LENT

Just as Jesus was tested before he started his formal ministry, it is right that Christians too should be tested to see whether they will be able to stand up to the difficulties of the Christian life.

Deuteronomy 26.1–11
Romans 10.8b–13
Luke 4.1–13

- 2 large sheets of paper marked 'Very tempted' and 'Not tempted'.
- Prit-tak or drawing pins.
- List of situations.
- Temptations Form for everyone.
- Pencils.
- Bowl.

□ *Starter*

Designate two different walls of your church as 'Very tempted', 'Not tempted' and put up large sheets of paper to remind everyone which is which. The walls should be reasonably accessible, with space in between for people to move. In a traditional church, therefore, they could be the east and west walls with the aisle connecting them.

Encourage people to leave their seats and to stand somewhere between the two walls, in a place that best reflects how tempted they feel by the following situations. For example, the more tempted they feel, the nearer to the 'Very tempted' wall they will stand. Remind them they are to be as honest as possible with their answers. Call out some of the following situations:

- A friend offers you fresh fruit or chocolate gateau for pudding. How tempted are you to opt for the gateau?
- You want to get out of going to see a relative because a friend has invited you to go to something better. How tempted are you to lie to get out of the first invitation?
- You see someone you find very irritating coming towards you; how tempted are you to cross over the road and pretend you haven't seen them?
- You've promised to do some more exercise by going running but it's pouring with rain. How tempted are you to put off the running until another day?
- It's a cold winter morning and you're in bed. How tempted are you not to go to church?
- You hear some 'juicy' information about someone you know. How tempted are you to pass on this piece of gossip?

TEMPTATIONS FORM

Two things that have tempted me in the past year:

1.

2.

One thing that is tempting me today:

□ *Comment*

In St Luke's Gospel we see Jesus being tempted by the devil. Having been acknowledged by his heavenly Father at his baptism and commissioned to start his work on earth, he now spends time alone in the wilderness to decide on the way he will carry out his ministry. Perhaps this story should be called the Testing of Jesus, rather than the Temptation of Jesus.

Just as a metal is tested for strength, or a car or other piece of new machinery is tested beyond its limits before it is used, Jesus is also tested. It would have been easy to use his power to draw people to him, but was this the best way to carry out his ministry? The 40 days and nights spent in the wilderness tested Jesus to the limit, though we are told he did not give in to the power of evil.

As Christians we too are frequently tested. It is not that God wants his people to give into temptation; that would be unthinkable. But it is right that as Christians we are tested. Like true metal we shall burn all the brighter. If we are faithful in the small temptations of this life, then surely we shall prove faithful in the larger challenges.

□ *Conclusion*

Before the service create a Temptations Form for every member of the congregation.

Give a Temptations Form, along with a pencil, to everyone in the congregation. Young children should work with adults. Allow a few moments for the forms to be completed, then collect the forms in a bowl. Offer the temptations at the altar with a suitable prayer.

THE SECOND SUNDAY OF LENT

St Paul says we are not citizens of this world, rather we are citizens of heaven, and as such we must learn to sit light to the things of this world.

Genesis 15.1–12, 17–18
Philippians 3.17—4.1
Luke 13.31–35

- Pictures of the good things in life.
- Lent Promise Cards.
- Paper.
- Pencils.

□ *Starter*

Create small groups of mixed-age people. Give each group a number of pictures cut from magazines, which show the good things of life (e.g. expensive toys, a computer, a large house, designer clothes, a beautiful room, a picture of a South Sea 'holiday' island), and ask them to use these to:

- Identify all the things of the world they enjoy.
- Identify what tempts them away from the things of God.

Allow time for contemplation and discussion. The group might want to jot down their thoughts on a piece of paper.

□ *Comment*

St Paul reminds the Philippians in his letter to them that they should follow his example in the way they live their lives. He complains that many people live as though they were enemies of Christianity. Instead of putting God first in their lives, the things of this world become more important. 'Their god is the belly,' he complains, and 'their minds are set on earthly things' (Philippians 3.19).

We too should remember that our home is in heaven, and we are citizens not of this world but of another. Instead of concentrating all our energies on getting the luxuries of life; or spending more than we can afford on clothes; or even giving all of our lives to our children, we should remember where our roots lie and put as much work into our Christian life.

As Christians belonging to another world, we need to learn to 'sit light' to this world, and learn to put more of our energies into developing our relationship with God and carrying out his work. This will bring eternal benefits.

□ *Conclusion*

Before the service create Lent Promise Cards for all the congregation.

In the space handwrite the following examples: 'Give more time to God', and 'Spend less on myself'.

Allow time for everyone to give some thought to what they might promise. Children should be encouraged to work with adults to think about ways in which they might change their lives during Lent. Encourage positive suggestions rather than negative 'giving up' ideas.

~ *Lent Promise Card* ~

As a citizen of heaven I promise to re-evaluate my priorities this Lent by:

THE THIRD SUNDAY OF LENT

Isaiah exhorts his listeners to 'Seek the Lord while he may be found', and this week we are encouraged to look for God both in our lives and in the rest of the world.

Isaiah 55.1–9
1 Corinthians 10.1–13
Luke 13.1–9

- Activity Sheets for everyone.
- Large cross.
- Small pieces of paper and pencils.
- Bowl.
- Bibles.
- Large limb of a tree in a pot.
- Photocopies of fruits.
- Lengths of string or wool.
- OHP or flip-chart.
- Fat felt-tip pen.

☐ *Starter*

Before the service create an Activity Sheet (see below) based on the readings, and produce sufficient copies for everyone. Place a large cross somewhere away from the altar, with pencils and small pieces of paper, and a bowl beneath; provide a large number of Bibles; put a large limb of a tree into a pot; photocopy a variety of pictures of 'fruits' (e.g. apples, pears, plums, etc.) leaving one side plain; place lengths of string or wool nearby, and provide pencils; and finally place small slips of paper on the altar together with some pencils.

Give out the Activity Sheet and invite people to work in pairs. Children should work with adults.

~ *Lent 3: Activity Sheet* ~

- Together look up the Old Testament reading (Isaiah 55 v 1 – 9) and read it. What does it say to you? Discuss with your neighbour.

- iscuss with your neighbour whether you have done anything special to mark Lent, and if so, how it's going. (If not, look at what you find special about Lent.)

- On your own, confess your sins by writing them down on a piece of paper and leaving them at the foot of the cross.

- Together look up the Gospel reading (Luke 13 v 1 – 9) and read it. Be honest with each other and look at the good things about yourselves. What are your fruits (e.g. love, joy, peace, patience, etc.)? Having decided, collect a fruit picture, and write your 'fruits' on it before hanging it onto the tree.

- Discuss with your neighbour what you would like to pray for. Collect a piece of paper and a pencil from the altar, write down your intercessions and place on the altar.

□ *Comment*

Like the seller in the market Isaiah calls his listeners to come and buy; to come and taste what is on offer. He derides them. Why do they spend what they possess on food which does not satisfy? Why do they seek for the things that will not last? Instead of being so short-sighted, he says, come and learn from God. For he is willing to make an everlasting agreement with his people purely because he loves them.

However, he also reminds them that not only must they look for things that are eternal rather than temporal, but they are to seek for the Lord while they can. There is a real sense of urgency in this passage. The invitation might not always be there, and we need to be alert to the opportunities as they arise. It's no use waiting until we are in trouble before we look to God, we need to search for him *now*, while he can be found.

Today we have looked at our Bibles to see what God is saying to us *at this moment*, we have given thought to the sins we wish to confess, and we have prayed for our world and for those around us. This is the weekly opportunity for seeking God, but there are many other such opportunities in our lives. We need to learn to make the most of these times, to 'seek the Lord while he may be found' (Isaiah 55.6).

□ *Conclusion*

Explore what other ways we can seek God. Invite people to turn to each other and find one or two ways in which they could seek God this Lent. Then hear back from everyone and put them up on an OHP or flip-chart. Remind the congregation they are to seek God 'while he may be found'.

THE FOURTH SUNDAY OF LENT:

MOTHERING SUNDAY

On Mothering Sunday we look at what it means to live together in a family as well as in the wider community, and at the give and take that is necessary for any family or community to be successful.

Joshua 5.9–12
2 Corinthians 5.16–21
Luke 15.1–2, 11b–32

- Copies of the Gospel reading.
- Copies of questions.
- Optional: The Dramatized Bible, 3 actors prepared to answer questions, and an OHP or flip-chart with a fat felt-tip pen.

□ *Starter*

Divide the congregation into groups of 6–8 people. Allocate a different character from the Gospel story to each group (father, elder son, younger son). Give each person a copy of the Gospel reading, and a copy of the questions. Invite the groups to read the story of the Prodigal Son again, but this time to look at it in relation to the person they are thinking about. Ask questions like:

- What might he like to say to his brother/father/son?
- What question(s) might he want to ask his brother/father/son?
- What might he feel like when his son/brother/he leaves home?
- What does the future hold for the younger son/elder son/father?

□ *Note*

Younger children might like to hear the story read from a children's Bible. Alternatively tell any story about a child who is jealous, or who is forgiven. Talk about the story with the children afterwards.

□ *Conclusion*

Gather the whole congregation together and encourage the groups to speak to one another, but to keep in character, e.g. 'I would like to say to my brother . . .', etc. If possible different groups should answer the queries and questions, e.g. 'The reason I left home was . . .'.

□ *Optional*

Before the service appoint three people to represent the three characters in the parable: the father, the elder son and the younger son. Read the story using the Dramatized Bible (those appointed may read the appropriate parts if desired), and then ask the whole congregation to think of questions to ask the characters in the story. These could be listed on a flip-chart or OHP. Finally put the characters on the spot and ask them to reply to the questions.

□ *Comment*

St Paul says we are ambassadors for Christ, and our ministry is one of reconciliation. This is no easy task, for we are actually to help reconcile people both to each other and to God. What does St Paul mean by the word 'reconciliation'? Perhaps we might like to think of it as bringing people together.

St Luke gives us a wonderful example of the difficulties that occur in any family situation. In this case it is a family of two sons and a father, but it might just as well be our church or village/town/estate community. The younger son with breathtaking audacity treats his father as though he were already dead and demands his share of the family property. We are not told, but presumably his father had to sell some of his land to achieve this. All of this the elder brother sees but can do nothing about. He simply goes on with his work.

As so often, Luke gives us a hero who is rather more of an anti-hero, for in the end he does the right thing for the wrong reason. He comes to his senses, because he finds himself longing for the food that is given to the pigs. However, it is his repentance that is at the heart of this story. No matter how wrong his actions, it is his wholehearted repentance that is to mend the relationship, so that when he returns home he finds his father already coming to meet him.

As Christians this parable reminds us of our own sin, and of the constant loving attitude of our heavenly Father towards us. But this story has another purpose. It teaches us something about the way we are to behave towards one another. The father is loving and understanding towards both his sons. Though he has been hurt he forgives the younger son and rejoices at his return. Later we see him going out to coax the elder son back to the feast and to effect a reconciliation with his brother. We too are called to forgive one another, to bring those who are upset back into the community, and to do all that we can to reconcile ourselves and those around us to a loving heavenly Father.

THE FIFTH SUNDAY OF LENT

This week sees the start of our preparations for Easter, as we are reminded that Jesus himself was prepared for the final part of his ministry of love.

Isaiah 43.16–21
Philippians 3.4b–14
John 12.1–8

- Bowl of water.
- Soap.
- Towel.
- Actors for a role-play.
- Cook and cook books.
- Parent to talk about preparation for Easter.
- 2 parents to talk about names for a new baby.
- Easter Preparation Card for everyone.
- Pencils.

□ *Starter*

In the week before ask a number of people to help with the service:

- 3 or 4 actors.
- A cook.
- A parent.
- 2 parents expecting a baby (or who have just given birth to a new baby).

Make sure they are well briefed, according to the instructions below.

In the service explain to the congregation that a number of activities are going to be carried out, and all of them have something in common with each other:

Activities
- Using a bowl of water, soap and a towel, invite one or two people to come forward and wash their hands.
- Conduct a short role-play of a family preparing to go on holiday. They should plan the route from home to their holiday destination, decide where they will stop for refreshments on the way, agree whether or not they will go by motorway, and arrange what time they will leave.
- Invite a cook to come forward carrying a number of cook books. They are to choose a menu, decide whether or not they have the ingredients in the pantry, make a list of what items they need to buy, and finally make a decision about what time they need to start cooking so the meal will be ready on time.
- Invite a parent to come forward and talk about Easter at their home: friends or family are coming to stay, the children therefore will need to share a room to make space for the guests, there is bed-linen to sort out, food to buy, and of course Easter eggs to get.

> - Invite two parents to come forward and discuss names for an expected baby. Should they choose family names, or something currently in vogue? How many names should they give the child, and what will they choose for a boy and for a girl?

When all the activities have finished invite everyone to turn to their neighbour and discuss what they think all the activities have in common. After a few moments invite everyone to make suggestions as to the answer. Finally encourage everyone to realize that they were all preparations for something else.

□ *Comment*

We wash our hands before we eat (or before we go out, or before we go to bed, or before we carry out any first aid); we prepare our route before we go away on holiday; we check our menu and our store-cupboard before we begin to cook the dinner; we plan for Easter and prepare the house before the family come to stay; and before our children are born we give much thought as to what we shall call them. All of these activities are about preparing for something else.

In the Gospel reading we have heard the story of Jesus at the house of Lazarus who lived in Bethany. Six days before the Passover Jesus joined the family, together with his disciples, for dinner and during the meal Mary took some expensive oil and anointed Jesus' feet. In a hot country like Palestine it was the custom to wash the feet of guests when they arrived in the house, but certainly not with costly oil.

However, just as Saul and David (see 1 Samuel 10.1 and 2 Samuel 2.1–4a) were anointed with oil before their accession as king, so Mary anoints Jesus before he too comes into his kingdom. In the same way that we prepare for many things in life, Mary prepares Jesus for the culmination of his three-year ministry. Just as kings of old were set apart for God's work, so Jesus is anointed and set aside for the task that lies ahead.

We too need to be prepared, not for the end of our ministry, but for the coming of Easter. During the six solemn weeks of Lent, we have, hopefully, observed our Lenten promises, but now we need to intensify our preparations so that when Easter comes we are ready to receive the Risen Lord into our lives once more.

□ *Conclusion*

Help the congregation to consider ways in which they might prepare for Easter. Give everyone a blank copy of the Easter Preparation Card (example on page 57), and encourage them to work in twos to discuss how they might approach Easter this year. Children should work with adults to find suitable ways of preparing themselves for Easter.

~ *Easter Preparation Card* ~

NAME: **MARY WALTERS**

In order to be prepared for Easter, spiritually, I will :

- Read about Jesus' death and resurrection.
- Attend a Maundy Thursday and/or Good Friday service.
- Read another Christian book.
- Carry out an act of service for someone else.
- Attend worship every day in Holy Week.

'God so loved the world, that he gave
~   his only begotten Son to the end that all   ~
who believe in him should not perish.'   John 3.16

PALM SUNDAY

Palm Sunday reminds us that the arrival of the king is imminent, and our preparation becomes even more important.

Psalm 118.1–2, 19–29   or   Isaiah 50.4–9a
Luke 19.28–40   Philippians 2.5–11
Luke 22.14—23.56 or Luke 23.1–49

- Outline of an imaginary kingdom.
- Paper for banners.
- Scissors.
- Pencils or pens.
- Glue.
- Paper for flags, and sticks.
- OHP or flip-chart, and fat felt-tip pen.

□ *Starter*

Ask the congregation to imagine that they are living in a kingdom called 'Peaceful' (or any other suitable name), ruled by King Stephen the Good. Create through your words an imaginary kingdom, e.g. the town or countryside in which they live; the kind of work they might do. The kingdom although fictitious can be as real as desired.

Then inform everyone King Stephen is coming to visit their village (or town) at the end of the month, and they are all members of the village (or town) council responsible for making this visit successful.

Divide the congregation into groups of 6–8 adults and children, and allocate the following tasks to different groups. Tasks can be duplicated if desired:

Tasks to welcome the king
- Create banners to welcome the king, with different slogans.
- Create flags to represent your country (these could be designed to represent the good things of the country – its people, its landscape, its industries etc.).
- Decide what places the king is to visit, e.g. a hospital, a school, and a factory? Are there any special projects of importance you feel he should visit, and why? Who should be on the welcoming committee, and who should be introduced to the king? If there is time, prepare a speech of welcome.
- The king is to visit your home. What will you do to prepare the home in the week or so before he comes? What would you want to show him? What would you not want to show him? Members should imagine King Stephen is to visit their own home in just over a week's time! What will you wear?
- The king is to visit your office block. As a group imagine what this important firm might be – does it have a name? What work does it do? How many does it employ? Where would the king be shown, and who would he meet? What is it important that he sees, and what would you prefer he didn't see? What work is there to do before King Stephen arrives next week? What will you wear?

Come back together again and share the results of all the work.
Display the banners and flags.

□   *Comment*

Palm Sunday heralds the beginning of Holy Week, and the pace of
the activity begins to speed up as Jesus and his disciples arrive at
Jerusalem. In St Luke's Gospel this journey has symbolically taken
some time, since chapter 9 in fact, and we are now at chapter 19!
Always the eyes of Jesus have been set on the long road to
Jerusalem, leading as we saw last week to his anointing as king by
Mary.

Now once more outside the village of Bethany, at the Mount of
Olives, he takes the next step and sends two of the disciples to fetch
a young colt. The text leaves it ambiguously unclear whether the
words mean 'God has need of the colt' or 'the Master [meaning
Jesus] has need of the colt'. But what we do know is that the animal
they fetch has never been ridden. It has, in a way, been set aside for
this sacred purpose.

Whether or not Jesus' arrival in Jerusalem was quite the
overwhelming event that films have portrayed is debatable. There
would have been many pilgrims gathering for the Passover, and it
was certainly customary to approach the Temple at some feasts
waving palms. But more importantly the disciples, perhaps looking
back later, saw the arrival of Jesus on a donkey as the fulfilment of
Zechariah's prophecy:

> Rejoice greatly, O daughter Zion!
> Shout aloud, O daughter Jerusalem!
> Lo, your king comes to you;
> triumphant and victorious is he,
> humble and riding on a donkey,
> on a colt, the foal of a donkey.
>   (Zechariah 9.9)

Zechariah's king is to be a king of peace. He is to bring in a reign of
peace. Ironically, Jesus the King of Peace, who comes to save his
people, also comes to meet his death at the hands of those who
cannot accept what he offers.

□   *Conclusion*

Using an OHP or flip-chart hold a discussion with the congregation
about Jesus who will come again to our homes and hearts as king at
Easter. Encourage everyone to suggest answers to the questions,
and link them to the work just done:

- When Jesus the king came to Jerusalem in what way did the people celebrate his entry? In what way do we celebrate the resurrection of Jesus Christ? We would welcome an earthly king with banners and flags, but how do we celebrate Easter and the King of Kings? (e.g. the decoration of our church, the inclusion of 'Alleluia' after the responses, the gathering of the whole family of God at church on Easter morning, etc.) Are there other ways that we could celebrate?
- When an earthly king comes to visit our village or town, we plan his itinerary, and the places he should visit. But if Jesus the king came to visit us, what would we want to show him, and what would we want to hide in our lives? Can we change this situation before next week (through confession, through putting something right, etc.)?
- An earthly king is introduced to a number of special people (perhaps because of their position in society, or the special job they do), but if Jesus the king came to visit, who might he want to meet? Will the list be different from that our group(s) made?

MAUNDY THURSDAY

Christians across the world celebrate the Eucharist, because of Jesus' command to 'Do this in remembrance of me'. Today's sermon slot looks at the different elements used in the Eucharist to explore the subject in more depth.

Exodus 12.1–4 (5–10)
1 Corinthians 11.23–26
John 13.1–17, 31b–35

- Facilitators for each group.
- List of readings.
- Bibles for everyone.
- Each group: A chalice with wine or blackcurrant juice, a paten (or plate) with a roll of bread, a towel, a bowl filled with water, a large sheet of paper, and a fat felt-tip pen.
- Copies of the questions for each facilitator.

☐ *Starter*

Divide the congregation into groups of 6–8 people. Gather
children into one or two groups suitable to their age, with an adult
facilitator (see work below). Give all the groups a chalice filled
with wine or blackcurrant juice, a paten with a roll of bread, a
towel, a bowl filled with water, a large sheet of paper, and finally
a fat felt-tip pen. The chalice and paten could be a goblet and a
small flat plate. If possible, everyone should have a Bible (these
can be any version, though preferably modern). Each group will
also need a facilitator, who should be given the list of readings,
and could have been given the task of gathering the items needed
for their group.

Place all the items gathered in the centre of the group. Then
invite members to 'brainstorm' words or images concerning the
items before them. Write everything onto the large sheet of paper.
The words or images might be of a specifically Christian nature,
but they could be more generalized. For example, the chalice might
bring to mind some of the following images:

wine
drink
blood
Jesus
death
communion service
remembrance
thirst

No suggestions are to be rejected by the facilitator. All should be
put onto the sheet of paper.

When the brainstorming has been completed the group is to
choose *either* to look at the readings concerning the bread and wine,
or the water and towel. Encourage everyone to look up the verses,
and ask different people to read them out loud.

Bread and wine	**Water and towel**
1 Corinthians 11.23–26	John 13.3–10
John 6.27	John 13.12–13
John 6.32–33	John 13.14–15
John 6.35	
1 Corinthians 10.16–17	
John 6.48–51	
John 6.53–57	
1 Corinthians 11.27–29	

□ *Conclusion*

Finally, consider the following questions in discussion:

Bread and wine

- What does Jesus mean by saying 'This is my body that is for you' and 'This cup is the new covenant in my blood'?
- Jesus says that we should receive bread and wine 'in remembrance' of him. How often do you think we should receive communion?
- When we receive the bread and wine we bring the past into the present, and approach the living God. How does this affect your life? (Those who do not as yet receive communion might consider what it ought to feel like.)

Water and towel

- Why do you think Jesus washed the feet of the disciples?
- What would be an equivalent action in today's world?
- How could members of your church show they truly love one another?

 □ *Optional*

Children's groups might like to explore the following reading and questions. Use a children's Bible.

Luke 22.1–20

- Jesus broke the bread and told his disciples that this broken bread was like his body. What was soon going to happen to Jesus' body?
- Jesus said we had to eat bread and drink wine to remember him. Do you think children should receive the bread and wine? If so, why, and at what age?

Lastly, the children might like to share the bread and drink the well-watered wine or blackcurrant juice (explain what this is, if it is used), as the story is read to them once more.

 □ *Comment*

At heart the Eucharist is simply a shared meal, but to Christians it is also so much more. Jesus shared a meal, probably the Passover meal, with his disciples. But at the end of the meal he introduced something that was entirely new. As we heard in our New Testament reading from 1 Corinthians:

> the Lord Jesus on the night when he was betrayed took a loaf of bread, and when he had given thanks, he broke it and said, 'This

is my body that is for you. Do this in remembrance of me.' In the same way he took the cup also, after supper, saying, 'This cup is the new covenant in my blood. Do this, as often as you drink it, in remembrance of me.' (1 Corinthians 11.23b–25)

With these words Jesus takes the covenant made between God and the Israelites at Mount Sinai, which was sealed with the blood of each male Jew at their circumcision, and changes it completely. This new covenant is to be made and sealed with the blood of Jesus himself. Since Jews dislike the thought of ever drinking blood and tried to ensure that all meat was free of it, this in itself must have been an amazing thought to the disciples. Blood was for them literally the 'life-blood' of a person or animal, so Jesus offers them a part of his life!

Jesus offers his body and his life-blood, for all people. In sharing in the Eucharist we reaffirm the new covenant made with God, and we share in the benefits.

GOOD FRIDAY

An exploration of the crucifixion stories in the Gospels leads to a fresh understanding of the way that different characters may have perceived the last week in Jesus' life.

Isaiah 52.13—53.12
Hebrews 10.16–25 or 4.14–16 or 5.7–9
John 18.1—19.42

- Editor and sub-editors.
- Copies of Bible readings and information for each sub-editor.
- A number of computers or typewriters.
- Large sheets of paper.
- Glue.
- A4 pack of paper.
- Scissors.
- Pens and pencils.
- Bibles.

□ *Starter*

Produce a copy of *The Jerusalem Times* for the first Easter. In the week before the service appoint an editor and a number of sub-editors. Each sub-editor should be responsible for a different section of the paper. The news sections will probably need a number of sub-editors, for example:

- News (Palm Sunday, Bethany and the woman who washed Jesus' feet, the Last Supper, Gethsemane, Trial, Crucifixion. Optional: The Resurrection).
- Religious Affairs (e.g. Pharisees, Sadducees, Herodians, Sanhedrin, chief priests, etc.).
- Foreign Affairs (e.g. Roman point of view, etc.).
- Women's Page (e.g. the Marys and other women who followed Jesus, etc.).
- Galilee (e.g. How would they see their local boy?).
- Politics (Pharisees, Romans, Sanhedrin, etc.).
- The Front Page.

Invite everyone to join a group. Each group is to prepare one or more pages for *The Jerusalem Times*:

News pages
Palm Sunday (John 12.12–16 or Matthew 21.1–11)
Overturning of the tables in the Temple, and healing of the lame (Matthew 21.12–14)
Bethany (John 12.1–8)
The Last Supper (John 13.1–30)
Gethsemane (Matthew 26.36–56)
Trial (Matthew 26.57—27.26)
Crucifixion (Matthew 27.15–60)
Optional: The Resurrection (Matthew 27.62—28.20)

Religious Affairs
Read Matthew 21.10–17; 23.1–33; 26.1–5; 26.47–68; 27.1–66; 28.1–5. Look at the events of Holy Week from the point of view of the Pharisees, the Sadducees, and the chief priests.

Foreign Affairs
Read Matthew 21.1–17; 21.23–46; 22.15–46; 27.1–2; 27.11–66; 28.1–15. Look at the events of Holy Week from the point of view of the Romans.

Women's Page
Read Matthew 26.6–13; 27.55–61; 28.1–10 (or Mark 15.40—16.8), John 19.25b–27; 20.1–18. Look at the events of Holy Week from the point of view of Mary the Mother of Jesus, Salome, Mary Magdalene, etc.

The Province of Galilee

Read John 12.1–8; Luke 19.29–48; 20.1–8; 21.37–38; chapter 22 to the end of chapter 24 as appropriate. Look at the events of Holy Week from the point of view of provincial Galilee and what they might think about their 'local boy', the carpenter from Nazareth.

Politics

Read Luke 19.29–48; 20.1–8; 20.44–47; 21.37–38; chapter 22 to the end of chapter 24, as appropriate. Look at the events of Holy Week from the point of view of the zealot party in Israel. At least one of Jesus' disciples was a zealot, who wanted to see Jesus start a revolution.

The Front Page

Read Mark 11.1–19; 14.3 to the end of chapter 16. Prepare a suitable front cover with artwork. This group could include a number of children, if desired.

Use a number of computers and printers if desired, or else use typewriters and stick-and-paste all material as it comes in. Each group will need to combine both facts from their reading with use of their imagination to create suitable 'news-style' articles. Include artwork, cartoons and adverts as desired. For a successful outcome give each person or small group a manageable task, and do not allow any one person to do all the work for one group.

☐ *Conclusion*

Put *The Jerusalem Times* together to form a newspaper. If desired, create further copies after the service for all the congregation, to be given out on Sunday.

☐ *Note*

Where time is short, leaders should prepare as much as possible beforehand. But why not extend the service on this day and enable everyone to spend more time on *The Jerusalem Times?*

☐ *Comment*

The Gospel accounts of the last week and the death of Jesus give us different pictures as they affect different people. Because we are familiar with the story of Holy Week, we have put all the different aspects together, forgetting that the story would have been seen differently by different sections of the community.

To the Galileans this would have been a story of local boy made good, coming to a dreadful end. The Pharisees and Sadduccees would have welcomed the death of Jesus, for he was considered to be a trouble-maker and blasphemer, while for those who followed Jesus his death was a stark tragedy.

Each of these groups also saw the resurrection in a different light, some welcomed it as a sign that the hand of God was at work in the world and some rejected it as being mere propaganda. Only when each separate part of the story is examined do we get the whole picture of the Easter story.

EASTER DAY

The good news of the resurrection of Jesus at Easter means that as Christians we are restored to a loving relationship with God, through repentance and forgiveness.

Acts 10.34–43 or Isaiah 65.17–25
1 Corinthians 15.19–26 or Acts 10.34–43
John 20.1–18 or Luke 24.1–12

- OHP or flip-chart and fat pen.
- Covenant forms for everyone.
- Pencils.
- Oil of chrysm.

☐ *Comment*

The resurrection of Jesus Christ brought with it the greatest possibility for change in the world. Up to the time of the death of Jesus, Jews were bound by the Law of Moses. They were constrained to obey the Law, or to fall short of God's wishes. They knew the impossibility of obeying the Law and because of this the Pharisees hedged the Law around with further laws, to ensure that no-one broke it inadvertently. Thus if the Law said 'you may not walk more than 5 miles on the Sabbath', they would invoke a rule saying 'no-one is to walk more than 4.8 miles on the Sabbath', to ensure they would always stay within the Law.

But no matter how hard a Jew tried, he could never entirely obey the Law and keep his covenant (or promise) with God. Always he fell short of what God desired. There seemed no way that he could be reconciled to God under Mosaic Law.

However, because of his perfect obedience even to death, Jesus makes a new agreement with God. Jesus acts as the go-between and bridges the gap between the Creator and his created beings. Now anything becomes possible, and we can be forgiven and restored once more to the place for which we were destined.

 ☐ *Starter*
Using an OHP or flip-chart and help from the congregation, list situations where the disciples, those mentioned in parables, or other characters in the Bible, might be said to have fallen short of God's standard and broken God's laws. For example:

Breaking God's Law
- Dives (in the story of Dives and Lazarus).
- King Herod.

 ☐ *Optional*
If desired, carry out this activity in small groups. You might want to give out Bibles.

 ☐ *Conclusion*
Before the service create copies of the following form for all the congregation:

THE NEW COVENANT
'Jesus died for me, and God forgives my sin.'

LIST THOSE SINS TO BE CONFESSED:

Give a copy of the form and a pencil to everyone, and encourage them to think back over the last few days before writing down their sins. Then conclude this section of the service by commenting that unlike those who made mistakes in the Bible and who could not be reconciled to God, our sins are forgiven by the reconciling power of God. As a symbol of our forgiveness anoint everyone's forehead or hands with holy oil and pronounce God's blessing using some simple words, e.g. 'God forgives you'.

☐ *Note*

Omit the penitential section of the service this week, as the sermon slot includes this.

THE SECOND SUNDAY OF EASTER

Like the apostles, we are called to be witnesses. We are called to testify to God's work in our lives.

Acts 5.27–32
Revelation 1.4–8
John 20.19–31

- 3 adults who are strangers to the congregation, one other adult from the congregation, and the minister, for the role-play.
- Copies of the Witness Statement for everyone.
- Pencils.
- OHP or flip-chart and fat pen.

☐ *Starter*

Create some role-play using two or three people that the congregation have never seen before. It might be possible to do this by speaking to neighbouring clergy and asking them to send over two or three members of their congregation to help. The visitors should be dressed in nondescript clothing, with at least one wearing a hat that hides their hair.

The role-play should involve the minister as follows:

Three men or women, all smartly dressed, knock on the minister's door. They say they are from the 'Heaven on Earth Trust', and have some good news for him/her and for the members of his/her congregation. Pleased, the minister invites the Trust members inside, and offers them a drink and a seat. Once settled the Trust members tell the minister why they have come.

Their Trust is responsible for offering churches a substantial sum of money to turn their church into the kind of building that everyone wants (e.g. with a kitchen, a toilet, a meeting room, a loop system for the hard-of-hearing, a churchyard that is a haven for wildlife, etc.). The members of the Trust are pleased to announce that the Trust has chosen the minister's church for their next project.

The minister is suitably impressed, even excited, and begins to talk about what can be achieved at St Ordinary's Church. He/she gets carried away, planning a rosy future for his/her church members, until one of the Trust members gently admits that there is a condition to the bequest. St Ordinary's Church will have to provide £1,000 as a down-payment to prove they are serious about the work that will be carried out.

The minister agrees to the request, still overjoyed at the project, and makes out a cheque for the amount required. The four shake hands on the bargain, and the Trust members leave promising to return by the end of the week with a cheque for the agreed money, so that the work can start immediately.

The Trust members leave, moving 'off-stage' to somewhere they cannot be seen. There is a pause before the minister's doorbell rings again. This time it is a policeman/woman. Having shown their identity card they are invited inside, where they proceed to tell the minister that he has been the subject of a con trick. The policeman tells him/her that this particular group of con-artists preys on clergy of all denominations, persuading them to give them £1,000, and in one case £5,000, in return for a generous bequest to modernize their church.

The policeman asks the minister for a description of the three people, and informs him/her that he might be needed as a witness at their trial if they are caught. He suggests that he might like to come down to the station to make the statement. The two exit talking about the 'heinous' crime!

 ☐ *Conclusion*
Before the service create copies of the form headed 'Witness Statement' (page 70).

WITNESS STATEMENT

	PERSON 1	PERSON 2	PERSON 3
Male or Female:			
Skin colour:			
Age:			
Height:			
Colour of hair:			
Distinguishing features:			

If the minister is conducting this part of the service he/she should return almost immediately. Now remind the congregation that they too were witnesses of this 'heinous' crime, and that you are going to ask them all to fill out a witness statement, describing the three members of the pseudo Trust.

Give out copies of the Witness Statement and pencils to everyone, and allow a few moments for them to fill in the form. Inform them that there should be no conferring, although adults may help young children who cannot read.

Then, using an OHP or flip-chart, ask the congregation for the results. You will need to identify the three people in some way, e.g. 'The man who spoke first', or 'The woman who took the cheque', etc. Take a head count on each question, and write the result on the board. For instance, how many thought the man who spoke first had brown hair, etc. Finally ask if anyone had any interesting comments to make under 'Distinguishing features'.

The results should predictably be very muddled. Now invite your visitors to return and check off their actual height/age/skin colour against the results. Conclude that 'Most of us wouldn't make good witnesses'.

 □ *Comment*
The disciples were witnesses to the life, death, and resurrection of Jesus, as God's Son. They were to take the good news of Jesus

throughout the world in the years after his death, to remember all that happened: the miracles that occurred; the parables Jesus told; and the response of the authorities to Jesus' teaching. Indeed the earliest disciples were to remember everything so accurately that their accounts mirror one another, as we can see in the first three Gospels (the Synoptic Gospels).

The disciples were lucky enough to see Jesus at work, but in today's Gospel reading Jesus commends those who believe, but who do not see. Thomas had not been with the disciples when Jesus first appeared, and despite the others telling him they had seen the Lord, he was not prepared to believe without laying down some conditions. He would not believe, he said, without being able to see the mark of the nails and the spear, and put his hands in the wounds. A week later Thomas has his chance and as a result Thomas greets Jesus with the words 'My Lord and my God!'

There is nothing wrong with Thomas' confession, but there had been something wrong with the way he had reached this conclusion. Thomas should have believed even without seeing Jesus. He should have believed because of the witness of the other disciples, and because of what he knew about Jesus. Blessed are those who will in future not see, but who will believe.

Today we have seen how difficult it is to witness to something – to remember actions, words, and description, and to be as accurate as possible. The task of a witness is two-fold. It is to remember *and* to tell others. As Christian witnesses we need to learn more about God as he works in our own lives, and we need to pass on our knowledge to other people by proclaiming the good news of Jesus Christ.

THE THIRD SUNDAY OF EASTER

Peter was told by Jesus to 'Feed my sheep'. As Christians we need to be fed spiritually, and as a church we are responsible for each other's growth and maturity.

Acts 9.1–6 (7–20)
Revelation 5.11–14
John 21.1–19

- OHP or flip-chart and fat pens.
- Paper and pencils or pens.

□ *Starter*

Explore the notion of health in our lives. Look at three different areas with the congregation, and think as widely round the questions as possible. Put all the suggested answers up on an OHP or flip-chart.

- What do babies need to stay healthy when they are first born? (e.g. warmth, food, sleep, stimulation, etc.)
- What things do children need to stay healthy as they grow up?
- What do adults need to stay healthy?

□ *Conclusion*

Using the information discovered about our physical health, look at how we might keep healthy, spiritually. Create small groups of no more than eight people, each with a group leader. There can be duplicate groups. Allocate the following activities:

1 Look at what babies and young children need to be nurtured in the faith. Consider their nurture in the faith, then draw up a Children's Charter. If possible take this to your church council and draw up a Charter agreed by everyone. Place on the church noticeboard.
2 Look at the position of parents with young children in your church. Draw up some practical guidelines or a leaflet, to help parents of young children.
3 Consider the nurture of teenagers. What do they need for healthy spiritual growth? Explore what work occurs in your church with teenagers. Draw up an ideal list of work that could be carried out with teenagers, and then compare with what does occur.
4 Look at the Christian nurture of adults. What do adults need for healthy spiritual growth? What Christian education is already taking place for adults in your church? Is it suitable for all adults? Could it be improved or extended? Draw up draft thoughts to put before your PCC or church council.
5 Look at the spiritual life of the group. Encourage everyone to look back over their lives, to discover what led them to having 'healthy' or 'unhealthy' times in their spiritual life. Be strict about ensuring that everyone has a chance to talk.

□ *Optional*

A children's group. Look at times when the children have been happy or unhappy. Does this always depend on material gifts or events? Have there been other times when they have been especially happy, perhaps because of people or places? Also look at how they feel about God and about the church.

☐ *Comment*

Jesus called on his disciples, and on Peter in particular, to 'Feed my sheep'. We have seen that as human beings we need to receive nourishing food, an appropriate amount of liquid, as well as shelter and protection, if we are to grow and mature. Everyone, whatever their age, needs certain conditions in which to stay healthy.

In the same way, as Christians, we need to receive the right spiritual nourishment, and the same careful nurture if we are to grow into mature Christians. For each of us the needs will vary slightly. But we do need to accept that each of us has needs. We can only continue to grow, spiritually, if these needs are met.

Jesus knew that his new church would need all the help and encouragement it could get. He knew that those who followed him would be tempted to stray, and he was concerned his new flock were fed the right kind of food. We too should be constantly aware of the needs of every Christian, whatever their age, and be careful to ensure whether we are thinking of toddlers, teenagers, or adults, we are meeting their spiritual needs within our church.

THE FOURTH SUNDAY OF EASTER

Jesus taught his disciples that just as the sheep knew the voice of the shepherd, so his people should know and recognize his voice.

Acts 9.36–43
Revelation 7.9–17
John 10.22–30

- A group of families.
- Blindfolds, if desired.
- Art materials.
- Newspapers, glue and large sheets of paper.
- Prayer and poetry books.
- Hymn books.
- Bibles.
- Paper and pencils.

☐ *Starter*

Arrange for up to 20 people to come forward from a number of different families. If the congregation is small in number fewer people could be chosen, but in this case there should be at least two people from every family. Invite one person of each family to be the 'caller', and ask the other members of the family to close their eyes or blindfold them.

Place the 'callers' in a large circle or square, with everyone else inside the circle. Ask the 'callers' to call the names of those in their family, using the most common name or nickname (possibly a diminutive used only in the family). The calling should all begin at the same time, and should continue until all those inside the circle have managed to find their family 'caller'.

In buzz groups of two or three discuss the following:

- Why is it possible to hear our own name over other people's voices?
- Why is it we can distinguish our own name, even if we become fairly deaf?
- Does it help to know the sound of the other person's voice?

 ☐ *Conclusion*

Working in small groups of no more than five or six people explore how we might know Jesus' voice. Any of the following ways could be used:

Art Group	After discussion produce a picture that shows ways in which the group might know the voice of Jesus at work in their lives.
Current News	Using as many current newspapers as possible, cut out stories that might be said to show 'the voice of Jesus at work today'. Paste the cuttings onto some large sheets of paper.
Prayer or poetry	Explore prayers or poetry concerned with 'the voice of Jesus'.
Hymns	Explore the words of hymns, and select five or six hymns that concentrate on 'the voice of Jesus'. If possible choose one, put a well-known tune to it if needed, and sing it later in the service. (This group will need at least one person who is capable of finding an appropriate tune that will fit the words.)
Reflection	Talk about a time when you knew Jesus was speaking to you.
Bible study	Look at stories in the Bible that might be said to teach us something about 'the voice of Jesus' (e.g. Martha and Mary, Luke 10.38–42; Jairus'

daughter brought back to life, Luke 8.40–42 and 49–56; the stilling of the storm, Mark 4.35–41; the healing of the paralysed man, Luke 5.17–26).

☐ *Comment*

Jesus uses the parable of the Good Shepherd to talk about his care for his people. The eastern way of caring for sheep relied on the sheep knowing the shepherd's voice as he came to lead them out of the fold in the morning. The good shepherd would lead his sheep, walking ahead to protect them. The good shepherd would lay down his life for his sheep. The good shepherd took care to find good pasture for the sheep. The good shepherd was recognized and followed by his sheep.

Similarly the sheep would listen out for the shepherd's voice and ignore the stranger; they would follow the shepherd but run away from the stranger. The sheep depended utterly upon the shepherd for their direction, their safety and their food.

Jesus says that he is the Good Shepherd and we are the sheep. We should know the voice of the Good Shepherd, and we should be prepared to follow wherever he leads. As we have seen, God speaks through many things in our world, we just need to be alert to his voice, and prepared to follow his wishes.

THE FIFTH SUNDAY OF EASTER

Jesus taught us to love one another, even as we love ourselves. What might this mean in practice?

Acts 11.1–18
Revelation 21.1–6
John 13.31–35

- Copies of the 'I Wish' list for everyone.
- Pencils and pens.
- Prit-tak or drawing pins.

□ *Starter*

Encourage everyone to spend a few moments creating an imaginary wish list, e.g. 'If I inherited a million pounds, I would . . .'. It may be as wild as they like. Ask everyone to turn and share their thoughts with their neighbour(s). Pause to listen to some of the wishes and share them with everyone.

Now inform the congregation they are to moderate their wish lists, to think of some more practical wishes. What two or three things would they like? Give examples, like 'someone else in the family to cook the Sunday dinner' or 'someone to wash the car' or 'someone else to walk the dog this week' or 'someone to read me a story'.

Give them a copy of the wish list form, prepared before the service, and a pen or pencil. Ask them to write down their wishes. Encourage children to work with adults.

I Wish...

1

2

3

Name:

□ *Conclusion*

Lastly gather in the wish lists and pin up where they can be seen. Spend time reading all the wish lists, and encourage everyone to carry out someone else's wish. Ideally everyone should be able to carry out one task for another member of the congregation, but since there may be elderly or very young children who cannot take part, it may mean some people will have to offer to complete two or three tasks. When each person has identified a task they are able to carry out they should tick it, and in the week(s) ahead arrange to carry out that wish for the other person. Tact will be needed on the part of both parties!

Leave the wish lists up for some weeks, if desired, and ensure that everyone has at least one wish carried out. There are no addresses on the lists for reasons of security, so others may have to help 'put different parties together'.

☐ *Comment*

Jesus' words to his disciples that they should 'love one another' are given in the form of a rule or command. This command was well-known to the disciples as we can see from the summary of the Law found in Mark 12.29 and 31, and was after all the basis of Jewish Law. The difference this time is that Jesus requires them to love one another as he loves them, and we know he loved them enough to suffer and die for them.

Jesus says by our behaviour to one another we shall be recognized as his disciples. Genuine, constant and self-sacrificing love for one another is the sign of being a Christian. The way we behave is to mirror our spiritual faith. Only then will Christians be able to influence the world around them.

So today we remind ourselves we should be showing a constant practical demonstration of God's love to those around us.

THE SIXTH SUNDAY OF EASTER

Jesus says those who love him keep his word. This week we try to apply his word to everyday situations.

Acts 16.9–15
Revelation 21.10, 22—22.5
John 14.23–29 or John 5.1–9

- Numbered sheets of paper, 1–50.
- Prit-tak or drawing pins.
- 2 judges.
- Question master.

- 2 players for each group.
- Dice or other means of choosing a random number.
- Pieces of paper and pencils.
- Questions.
- Optional: Game of snakes and ladders, dice, and questions for children.

☐ *Starter*

Before the service place numbered sheets of paper around the church in order, from 1 to 50. Then create groups of up to six people (with duplicate groups if necessary). Each group should then spend 3 or 4 minutes discussing the following question:

> Jesus says, 'If anyone loves me he will keep my word.' If we are to obey Jesus we need to apply 'his word' to everything in our lives. Can you come up with one or two simple laws to use that would help you apply 'his word' to situations?

Next appoint two judges, and one question master. Each group should nominate two people as Players in 'The Game of Life'. Decide in what order the different groups will start the game, then roll a large dice (or use some other suitable means of choosing a random number from 1 to 6). The first pair of players should then move to the appropriate sheet of paper (e.g. roll a 5 and move to sheet no. 5). The question master then asks the pair the *first question* on the question list below. (Groups might want to write down their questions!) One player should return to her or his group to get help in answering the question, the other (possibly a child) should stay by the numbered sheet as a 'counter'.

While the first group are deciding upon an answer to the question, the game continues. The dice is rolled and the next pair of players moves. When a group have an answer ready they should ask the judges to decide how good the answer is. Judges have the power to send a pair of players backwards or forwards, and the game will be more fun if the judges use this power.

> 1 There are many laws (Christian/law of the land etc.). Which do you think are the three most important?
> 2 You have won £75,000 – what will you do with it?
> 3 When bringing up a child which three rules might be important?
> 4 When thinking about choosing a career, which precepts might guide you?

5 When keeping the peace between your three children, which two things might be important to remember?

6 You have a gap year. List your choices of where to go in order of preference.

7 Which three things are important to you when choosing a school for your child?

8 You have four hours free time every week. What could you do with them? Give four suggestions.

9 Someone asks you if the clothes they are wearing look OK. In your opinion they look dreadful. What do you say?

10 You decide to do three things to help the environment. What would they be, and in which order of preference?

Make up more questions if needed. Continue the game until someone reaches sheet no. 50.

☐ *Comment*

As Christians we need to live our lives according to some rules. Although we have the Ten Commandments, it is not always easy to apply these to some situations in life. Ultimately we need to apply Jesus' words to 'love God and our neighbour' as best we can when dealing with our children, our work and our leisure.

Sometimes there are no clear answers, as we have seen. Today we have applied Jesus' words to imaginary situations and we haven't had to carry them out for real. Perhaps if we actually won £75,000, we would find it more difficult to give it away.

Jesus says those who love him will keep his word, and that he and the Father will come and 'make our home with them' (John 14.23). With this promise in mind when we are faced with a difficult decision, all we can do is to try and measure it against Jesus' words about love, and ultimately to pray for guidance. We will not always be right, but we can try to live by rules which have a Christian basis, rather than make decisions based on whim or on our mood at the time.

☐ *Conclusion*

Discuss with the whole congregation the difficulties of answering the questions, and of how easy or difficult it might be if the situations were real.

☐ *Optional*

Take younger children into a group of their own and play a 'table-top' version of snakes and ladders, asking simple questions of each child every time the dice is thrown. For example:

1 John has just hit you, should you hit him back?

2 Mary has broken your best doll/car; should you break one of her toys? etc.

ASCENSION DAY

The disciples were commanded by Jesus to take the message of salvation to the world. Our task as those who have heard God's word is to pass it on to others.

Acts 1.1–11 or Daniel 7.9–14
Ephesians 1.15–23 or Acts 1.1–11
Luke 24.44–53

- Unwanted rolls of wallpaper.
- Scissors.
- Felt-tip pens.
- Washing-line.
- Pegs.

☐ *Comment*

St Luke describes Jesus' last appearance to the disciples as coming hard on the heels of the resurrection. Jesus appears to them while they are all together, listening to the words of the two men who had accompanied him on the walk to Emmaus. He confounds them by proving he is no ghost. He asks them to touch him 'for a ghost does not have flesh and bones' (Luke 24.39b), and then eats a piece of broiled fish.

But his last session with the disciples is primarily taken up with teaching them about God's purpose for the world. It was written, he says, that the Messiah should suffer and rise on the third day. Then he continues by giving them the Great Commission. They are to go out into the world to proclaim 'repentance and forgiveness of sins . . . in his name to all nations' (Luke 24.47). As witnesses of all that has happened, their work now is to go to the whole world, starting with Jerusalem, and to preach repentance.

Of all the commands given to us by Jesus, this is probably the most important. It was the only command he gave to the disciples before he withdrew from them and returned to the Father. Yet it is a command that Christians seem to find hard to follow. Today we are called to announce that a change of heart is necessary. We are not called to preach 'Woe', but love. God desires to forgive his people. All that is needed is for his people to acknowledge their guilt. Our job is to tell the world around us there is a God who loves all his people, and that he wants them to turn again to him.

□ *Starter*

Divide the congregation into small mixed-age groups. Give each group one or two rolls of unwanted wallpaper (of any colour or pattern), a number of scissors, and some felt-tip pens. The groups are to be given the task of drawing around all the people in the group. Unroll the wallpaper and lay it flat on the floor with the front of the paper upwards (the plain back will become the front). Lay members of the group down on the paper, draw round them one at a time, and then cut out their silhouettes. Try to persuade everyone to have their silhouette drawn. In any event make sure there is one silhouette for each member in the group as well as one spare one.

□ *Conclusion*

When the silhouettes are cut out invite everyone to write their name onto the 'front' (the plain side) of one of the cut-out figures, and to remember they are one of the people who have been brought to Christ; they are one of the people whom God loves; and they are one of the people who have confessed their sin *and* been forgiven.

Now ask everyone to think of someone who still needs to hear the news that God loves them. Who needs to hear that God wants them to change, and that he is longing to forgive them? When they have thought of someone write just their Christian name on the spare silhouette.

Place all the silhouettes round the church. If there is only a small amount of wall space hang 'washing lines' up and peg the silhouettes onto them, close together.

Finally remind everyone that all these 'people' represent both those who have heard Jesus' words *and* those who have not heard his message. The job of those who have heard Jesus' words is to pass the words onto those who have not heard them. Our job is to pass the news onto the people we have named on our silhouettes, and to do that we can start with prayer for them.

□ *Note*

Include in the service prayers for the church, all Christians, and those who have yet to repent and be forgiven.

THE SEVENTH SUNDAY OF EASTER

Jesus prays that his disciples may be one with him and with his Father. To be 'one with the Father' indicates that we have something in common with him, as children take after their parents.

Acts 16.16–34
Revelation 22.12–14, 16–17, 20–21
John 17.20–26

- List of organizations and groups.
- OHP or flip-chart, paper and fat pens.
- Large life-size picture of a person.
- Small pictures of a person and pencils.
- Optional: A family prepared to talk about their similarities.

☐ *Starter*

Set up mixed-age groups of between 6–8 people. Instruct each group to decide what the members of the following clubs and organizations might have in common with one another. Allocate one organization to each group:

- Guides.
- School.
- Brownies.
- Fire service.
- Scouts.
- Ambulance workers.
- Cubs.
- Army.
- Hospital workers.
- Cricket team.
- Air Force.
- Football team.
- Navy.
- Drama club.
- Jury.

Example: Members of the Mothers' Union may have the following in common:

- Members are Christians.
- Members support the MU Aims and Objectives.

- Members have been admitted to membership.
- Members pay a subscription.
- Members meet together for worship.
- Members subscribe to the *Home and Family* magazine.

Allow time for discussion and then look at some of the results, briefly.

☐ *Optional*

Explore the similarities in a family between members. Before the service invite a family to think about their similarities, and to share them with the congregation, e.g. hair colour, eye colour, shape of head, way they walk, size, interests, etc.

☐ *Conclusion*

Put up a large picture of a human being on an OHP or flip-chart. This is to represent each person present. Consider what Christians might have in common with their heavenly Father. Jesus says we are made in God's image. What does this mean? Write up answers around the figure as they are given.

Then look at whether there are other similarities we would *like* to possess? Encourage the congregation to think about Jesus and his relationship with God. Write any suggestions on the OHP or flip-chart.

Before the service create a small picture of a human being (see page 83). Give a copy to each person together with a pencil. Encourage everyone to write the ways in which they hope to improve themselves so they become more like God. These should be taken home and worked on. Refer to them at a later stage in the year, reminding the congregation of their desire to grow more like their heavenly Father.

☐ *Comment*

As we have seen, organizations and people often have much in common. Organizations have rules and regulations, uniforms, and mutual goals that hold them together. Similarly families who care for one another are families that will stay together.

The unity of the Trinity has something of both these aspects. Father, Son and Holy Spirit have a unity that is entirely voluntary and is characterized by the desire to glorify each other. It is the Father's pleasure to glorify the Son, and the Son's to glorify the Father. In his turn Jesus passes on all that he has from the Father to the disciples, and through them to a wider world. It is a life lived in pure love.

As Christians we reflect God's love when we live in love with one another, free from conflict or disagreement. We don't have to live the same kind of lives, do the same kind of jobs, or even like the same kind of things, but we do have to live and work together in love. Love is the secret ingredient that unites us to each other and to God.

DAY OF PENTECOST

What difference did the coming of the Holy Spirit make to the disciples, and what difference can he make to our own lives?

Genesis 11.1–9
Acts 2.1–21
John 14.8–17 (25–27)

- Paper.
- Pencils.
- OHP or flip-chart.
- Fat pen.
- My Faults form for everyone.
- List of texts for groups.
- Bibles for everyone, if possible.

☐ *Starter*

In small mixed-age groups explore the disciples' actions before and after Pentecost. Allocate a disciple (e.g. nominate one group John, and another Simon, etc.) and some of the appropriate readings to each group. Where there are a number of readings for a disciple spread them across two or more groups, and if desired give a group two disciples where there is little known about them, so that they can see the difference before and after Pentecost. There can be duplicate groups, if necessary.

Simon Peter

Before Pentecost: Matthew 14.22–33 (walking on water); Matthew 16.13–20 (profession of faith/keys of heaven); Matthew 18.21–22 (forgiveness of sins); Mark 8.31–33 (first prophecy of the passion); Mark 13.1–4 (questions); Luke 5.1–11 (fishers of men/large catch); Luke 9.28–36 (Transfiguration); Luke 22.31–34 (denial foretold); Luke 22.54–62 (Peter's denial); John 13.1–16 (washing of feet); John 18.1–11 (cutting off of the servant's ear); John 21.15–17 (Feed my sheep). *After Pentecost*: Acts 2.14–23 (speech); Acts 3.1–10 (cure of lame man); Acts 4.5–22 (before the Sanhedrin); Acts 9.32–35 (healing); Acts 9.36–43 (healing); Acts 10.44–48 (Holy Spirit received); Acts 12.1–17 (escape from prison).

Andrew

Before Pentecost: Matthew 4.18–20 (Follow me); Mark 13.1–4 (questions); John 6.1–15 (miracle of the loaves and fishes).

James

Before Pentecost: Matthew 4.21–22 (Follow me); Mark 10.35–45 (who is the greatest?); Mark 13.1–4 (questions); Luke 9.51–56 (Samaritan village inhospitable).

John

Before Pentecost: Matthew 4.21–22 (follow me); Mark 10.35–45 (who is the greatest?); Luke 9.49–50 (using the name of Jesus); Mark 13.1–4 (questions). *After Pentecost*: Acts 3.1–10 (cure of lame man); Acts 4.5–22 (before the Sanhedrin).

Matthew
Before Pentecost: Matthew 9.9 (Follow me).

Thomas
Before Pentecost: John 14.1−7 (don't know where you're going);
John 20.24−29 (doubts).

Nathaniel
Before Pentecost: John 1.43−51 (doubts anything good from
Nazareth).

Philip
Before Pentecost: John 6.1−15 (miracle of the loaves and fishes);
John 14.1−10 (questions about the Father). *After Pentecost*: Acts
8.1−8 (in Samaria); Acts 8.9−13 (conversions); Acts 8.26−40.

Judas
Before Pentecost: John 14.21−23 (questions).

Disciples
Before Pentecost: Matthew 8.23−27 (calming of the storm);
Matthew 13.10−14 (why speak in parables?); Mark 9.14−29
(failure to heal demoniac); Mark 9.33−37 (dispute about who is
the greatest?); Luke 18.15−17 (turning away children); Luke
22.39−46 (disciples sleeping); John 6.16−21 (Jesus walking on
water); John 9.1−7 (cure of man born blind); John 16.16−20
(questions). *After Pentecost*: Acts 2.37−47 (belief together); Acts
2.42−47 (living together); Acts 4.32−35 (early life together); Acts
5.17−21 (a miraculous deliverance from prison); Acts 6.7 (spread
of mission); Acts 9.31 (building up of the church).

Give everyone a copy of a Bible (any version, though preferably a
modern one), some paper, a pencil, and a copy of the list of texts.
Groups are to consider the following question when looking up the
texts concerning their disciples(s):

• What are the principal differences between the actions and
  behaviour of the disciple(s) before and after receiving the Holy
  Spirit?

If desired list the differences to action and behaviour; alternatively
think of words that describe the differences, e.g. cowardly, brave,
etc. Before proceeding, hear back from each group. Is it possible to
create a 'picture' of a disciple *after* he has received the power of the
Holy Spirit?

☐ *Conclusion*
With the whole congregation consider 'our faults'. Using an OHP
or flip-chart create a huge list of possible faults. Then give everyone
a sheet headed 'My Faults' and a pencil, and ask them to complete

it putting in those faults that are appropriate to them. Gather the sheets together and offer at the altar when the offertory or intercessions occur. Make sure they are anonymous, and are shredded or burnt afterwards.

☐ *Comment*

As we have seen, the coming of the Holy Spirit made a huge difference to the disciples. Before the coming of the Holy Spirit they seemed relatively powerless. We see examples of them unable to heal a boy without the help of Jesus, asking ignorant questions, jumping in without thinking, and of falling asleep when Jesus has his greatest need of them. They are very much learners prior to Jesus' death. Without his help they get into trouble.

But the arrival of the Holy Spirit changes all that. The Spirit fills them with confidence, with knowledge, and with power. No longer are they cowering, timid men. Almost immediately we see Peter and then Stephen arguing fluently that Jesus is both Lord and Messiah, and the people should acknowledge him as such. Stephen goes to his death in the calm certainty that he is in God's hands and all is well. A few days later Peter and John faced with the lame man at the Beautiful Gate confidently stretch out their hands and say:

'I have no silver or gold, but what I have I give you; in the name of Jesus Christ of Nazareth, stand up and walk'

and the man is healed (Acts 3.6).

The Holy Spirit is the power of God in our world today, and can and does make such changes in the lives of ordinary people. At our baptism (and confirmation) we received the Holy Spirit. Let us remember that with his help we too can confidently carry out God's work.

TRINITY SUNDAY

The theme for today encourages an exploration of the different aspects of the Trinity, and looking at the relationship of the Father, the Son, and the Holy Spirit helps us to explore our relationships with each other.

Proverbs 8.1–4, 22–31
Romans 5.1–5
John 16.12–15

- 3 very large 'graffiti boards'.
- Felt-tip pens for everyone.
- Paper for everyone.
- Leader, helper, and children's Bible.

□ *Starter*

Create three huge 'graffiti boards' and put them up in church. Make sure the boards come down low enough for small children to write or draw on them, but are wide enough to allow maximum access by people. Give each board a title: 'Father', 'Son', 'Holy Spirit'.

Give everyone in the congregation a sheet of paper and a felt-tip pen. Then ask them to think for a moment in silence about *one* of the three parts of the Trinity: the Father, the Son, or the Holy Spirit. When they have given some thought, they are to jot down as many words that come into their heads as possible. For example 'the Son' might elicit: man, God, Jewish, kind, etc. Parents should work with children who cannot write, so rather than silence there may be a quiet murmur in church. Finally, ask everyone to write *one or two* (not all) of their thoughts on the correct graffiti board.

Repeat this twice more until everyone has completed something on all three parts of the Trinity.

□ *Note*

Younger children could be read some short stories during this time, about God the Father, about Jesus, and about the Holy Spirit, e.g. God creating the world; a story based on the life of Jesus; and the coming of the Holy Spirit at Pentecost. These may be from a children's Bible. Talk in a very simple way about God being three-but-one – in the same way that if we look at one another from behind or face on or sideways we may look different, but we are still the same person.

□ *Comment*

Today we are looking at one of the most difficult concepts in Christianity: God as Trinity. We have all heard different ways of explaining the Trinity – the idea of the clover leaf, with three separate segments which make up one whole leaf; or the mathematical notion of $1 \times 1 \times 1 = 1$. But nevertheless it can be difficult to take in the idea, not least because we are brought up with the knowledge there is *one* God.

Our Gospel reading gives us another insight into the Trinity. Jesus says all that God possesses belongs to him, and in turn, the Holy Spirit's work is to glorify all that Jesus does. To our mind this is also strange. But perhaps we can simplify their relationship.

The three persons of the Trinity (and we must note the Holy Spirit is a *person* not an *it*) exist in a voluntary relationship of love, seeking only to show each other in glory. We might say they seek only to help each other and to make each other even better.

We speak of 'blowing our own trumpet', but the nearest equivalent of the relationship between the Trinity would be 'blowing another's trumpet'. When we seek to encourage others, to bolster flagging confidence, or to work for the good of someone else, then we too are living in a trinitarian way.

 ☐ *Conclusion*

Carry out one of these two activities:

1 Discuss the previous activity:
   - Which aspect of God was the hardest to write about?
   - Which was the easiest to write about?
   - Was it easy or difficult to choose just one or two things to say?
   - (look at the boards) Did we say the same things?
   - Is there anything unusual we need to comment on?
2 Invite the congregation to walk around the church. Play quiet music to cover the sound of feet. When anyone meets another person, they should stop and say something affirmative about the other. Don't give examples unless necessary, but if everyone looks baffled suggest a nice comment on their appearance or a positive comment on something they have recently done, etc.

PROPER 4

Sunday between 29 May and 4 June inclusive (if after Trinity Sunday)

The Christian is a person under authority, he or she is a servant of God. As God's servants, we should be bold enough to ask for his help.

1 Kings 18.20–21 (22–29) 30–39
Galatians 1.1–12
Luke 7.1–10

> - 4 people to hold placards.
> - 8 placards, written on both sides.
> - A story-teller.
> - Someone to conduct the 'sound effects'.
> - OHP or flip-chart and fat felt-tip pen.

☐ *Starter*

Before the service create eight placards, four for each group. They need to be large enough to be seen by each group, and should be produced back-to-back. Write the following instructions on them:

Placard 1 (for Group 1):   Grumble, grumble!
Placard 2 (for Group 1):   Go away! Get lost!
Placard 3 (for Group 1):   We don't want to know!
Placard 4 (for Group 1):   Yahweh is God! Yahweh! Yahweh!
Placard 5 (for Group 2):   Jeering laughter
Placard 6 (for Group 2):   Yeah! Yeah! Hurrah!
Placard 7 (for Group 2):   Boo! Boo!
Placard 8 (for Group 2):   Hear us, Master! Hear us!

Divide the congregation into two groups. The groups are to play the following parts:

Group 1   Israel
Group 2   Prophets of Baal

Appoint four people to act as placard holders, and instruct them to hold up the placards *when the text is needed* in front of their group, so they can read them out at the appropriate time in the story. Also appoint a conductor who has the full script and informs the placard holders which words to hold up using a baton or stick.

Tell the congregation the two groups are different people in the story, and you expect them to help you by making suitable sound effects as shown on the placards. If necessary have a practice. The story-teller should *pause* at the points where the sound effects occur, before continuing. Explain that 'Yahweh' is the name for God, as given to Moses in the desert.

Finally tell the story of Elijah and the prophets of Baal (1 Kings 18):

> Ahab, the king, called all the people of Israel to come before him on Mount Carmel. (*Group 1: Grumble, grumble!*) Then he demanded the presence of the prophets of Baal (*Group 2: Jeering laughter*) and also Elijah the prophet.
>
> When all the people had assembled, Elijah stepped forward to speak to them. (*Group 1: Go away! Get lost!*) Elijah stared angrily at them. The people continued to complain. What did Elijah

want? (*Group 1: Grumble, grumble!*) They were fed up with him moaning at them. (*Group 1: Grumble, grumble!*) The other prophets simply laughed at him. (*Group 2: Jeering laughter*)

Elijah stared at the people. (*Group 2: Jeering laughter*) 'How long do you mean to shilly-shally, before making up your mind who is God?' he cried. 'If you believe Baal is god, follow him! (*Group 2: Yeah! Yeah! Hurrah!*) On the other hand if you believe that Yahweh is God, follow him!' (*Group 2: Jeering laughter*)

But the people were silent, not saying a word. Elijah continued. 'I, alone, am the only prophet of Yahweh left. (*Group 2: Jeering laughter*) Look at the prophets of Baal, there are 450 of them! Let us have a trial of strength between us to decide who is Almighty God. (*Group 2: Yeah! Yeah! Hurrah!*) If Yahweh is God then I shall win.'

At this the prophets of Baal laughed all the more. (*Group 2: Jeering laughter*) The chief prophet shouted back, 'What do you think your God Yahweh can do? Baal is the only god,' he shouted. (*Group 2: Boo! Boo!*)

Elijah ignored the prophets. 'You're just afraid that Baal isn't up to it!' he taunted them. (*Group 2: Jeering laughter*) (*Group 1: We don't want to know!*) 'Come on! What about a trial of strength?' shouted Elijah, laying down his challenge. 'Let each of us lay the wood for a fire, prepare a bull for the sacrifice on top, and see which God can light the fire.' (*Group 2: Jeering laughter*)

The prophets of Baal prepared the fire and placed the bull on top. Then they called on their god, Baal, to help. (*Group 2: Hear us, Master! Hear us!*) They kept this up for hours but Baal did not answer them. Finally at midday Elijah spoke. 'Cry some more!' he jeered. 'Perhaps he's sleeping!' (*Group 2: Jeering laughter*)

Then the prophets of Baal called even louder. (*Group 2: Hear us, Master! Hear us!*) And they even cut their arms and their legs until the blood spouted, but there was no reply from Baal.

Finally Elijah spoke to the people. (*Group 1: Grumble, grumble!*) 'Come here,' he said. (*Group 1: We don't want to know!*) 'I will show you how powerful Yahweh is!'

Then he repaired the Lord's altar which had been destroyed. (*Group 2: Boo! Boo!*) He ignored the prophets of Baal, and restored the altar using 12 stones to represent the 12 tribes of Israel. (*Group 2: Jeering laughter*) Then he dug a deep trench around the altar. (*Group 2: Jeering laughter*) Finally, he filled four jars full of water and poured it onto the bull, the wood, and the stones. The prophets of Baal jeered even more (*Group 2: Boo! Boo!*), and the people of Israel began to murmur even more. (*Group 1: Grumble, grumble!*) But Elijah simply continued pouring even more water on the sacrifice. (*Group 2: Jeering laughter*) Three times he did this, so that the water ran from the altar, into the trench.

Finally the people grew silent, and even the prophets of Baal began to watch as Elijah knelt to pray. 'Lord God, the God of Abraham, Isaac, and Israel, show yourself as God of Israel. Let it be known that I have done these things at your request, and that you alone are God.'

Elijah stepped back, and as he did so a flame fell from the sky. (*Group 1: Yahweh is God! Yahweh! Yahweh!*) The flames burnt up the wood, the stones, the bull and even the water in the trench. The people and the prophets of Baal began to shout. (*Group 2: Hear us, Master! Hear us!*) (*Group 1: Yahweh is God! Yahweh! Yahweh!*) Then finally the people fell on their faces before Elijah and acknowledged that Yahweh was God!

 □ *Comment*

The people of God in the Old Testament story had deserted God's ways and ignored his commands. They treated Elijah, and the other prophets, in a shameful way. At the instigation, initially, of Jezebel who was attempting to bring the worship of the Phoenician god Melkart into Israel, the people had begun to worship Baal and Asherah. The situation was made worse with the encouragement of King Ahab who began to persecute the prophets of God.

Finally of all the prophets of God there is only Elijah left to stand up to the people and their heathen gods, and it is at this point that he stages the most incredible public showdown. If God is really the only god then he can do anything, thinks Elijah. He can even provide the fire for a sacrifice which has been drenched in buckets of water. And so he challenges the prophets of Baal to show what their god can do, and when they fail he stage-manages the setting up of a sacrifice that should under no ordinary circumstances be able to burn.

For Elijah there is no other way to show the people the incredible power of the Almighty God. He does not hesitate, for he has no doubts that Yahweh will succeed where the other gods fail.

 □ *Conclusion*

In small groups consider what 'gods' we worship today, e.g. money, work, golf, etc. Encourage people to be honest about themselves and about society. Explore with any children when it might be considered to be a bad thing to put all our effort into the things of this world (e.g. how much time do they spend watching television or playing on the computer?), so that these things become idols.

Hear back from the groups and put the results onto an OHP or flip-chart.

PROPER 5

Sunday between 5 and 11 June inclusive (if after Trinity Sunday)

St Paul argues that God set him apart and called him for his task. From our birth God is with us, there is nowhere we can go that is beyond his reach.

1 Kings 17.8–16 (17–24)
Galatians 1.11–24
Luke 7.11–17

- Copies of Psalm 139, for each group.
- Fat felt-tip pens.
- Large sheets of paper.

☐ *Starter*

Read Psalm 139.1–18; 23–24 aloud:

Lord, you examine me and know me,
you know if I am standing or sitting,
you read my thoughts from far away,
whether I walk or lie down, you are watching,
you know every detail of my conduct.

The word is not even on my tongue,
Lord, before you know it altogether;
close behind and close in front you fence me round,
shielding me with your hand.
Such knowledge is beyond my understanding,
a height to which my mind cannot attain.

Where could I go to escape your spirit?
Where could I flee from your presence?
If I climb the heavens, you are there,
there too, if I lie in Sheol.*

If I flew to the point of sunrise,
or westward across the sea,
your hand would still be guiding me,
your right hand holding me.

* *Sheol means the place of the dead.*

If I asked the darkness to cover me,
and light to become night around me,
that darkness would not be dark to you,
night would be as light as day.

It was you who created my inmost self,
and put me together in my mother's womb;
for all these mysteries I thank you:
for the wonder of myself, for the wonder of your works.

You know me through and through,
from having watched my bones take shape
when I was being formed in secret,
knitted together in the limbo of the womb.

You had scrutinized my every action,
all were recorded in your book,
my days listed and determined,
even before the first of them occurred.

God, how hard it is to grasp your thoughts!
How impossible to count them!
I could no more count them than I could the sand,
and suppose I could, you would still be with me.

God, examine me and know my heart,
probe me and know my thoughts;
make sure I do not follow pernicious ways,
and guide me in the way that is everlasting.

Now divide the congregation into small mixed-age groups. Allocate each group a verse (or two) of Psalm 139, some large sheets of paper and a number of *fat* felt-tip pens of different colours.

The task for each group is to look at the verse(s) they have been given, and decide what that means for them. Ask questions like:

- Have you ever felt 'searched out' by God?
- Does God 'know' you?
- Do you 'know' God?

Come to some group decisions about what the verse means for everyone, and then decide how this can be shown in *picture* form.

As a group make a large 'outline' picture to represent the verse(s) given to the whole group in bold strokes, with a fat felt-tip pen. This can be drawn by one person, but the whole group should be involved in the decisions about the picture.

 □ *Comment*
In the New Testament reading today we see St Paul writing to the Christians in Galatia about his conversion. He tells them how

zealous he was in persecuting the church of God and in trying to destroy it, in order to support the traditions of his ancestors. As a Pharisee he would have seen it as his duty to protect the Jewish traditions of his forefathers, and the Christian sect would have been like a red rag to a bull!

However, it is at this point in Paul's life that Jesus reveals himself to him, for we know while travelling to Damascus he encounters Christ. From this moment on Paul's life changes and instead of persecuting the church, he does all that he can to build up the lives of the believers.

In the letter to the Galatians, however, Paul says that God set him apart before he was born (Galatians 1.15). He also argues that God called him from before he was born. In Psalm 139 we see the same thought. God is with us from before our birth, even while we are in the womb. There is nowhere we can go where he will be absent. Whether we travel to the farthest reaches of the earth or the universe, God will be there. Whether we travel under the earth or the seas, indeed whether or not we turn our backs on him, he will still be there.

For some this might seem a rather scary thought (that God is always with us), but it should not be so. God is the source of all love. God has nothing but a desire to love us, and for us to respond to him in love.

□ *Conclusion*

Read Psalm 139 again, this time slowly, and as each verse is read hold up the relevant pictures.

□ *Optional*

Ask each group to read their verse, hold up their picture, and explain their thinking. This should be done before reading the psalm for the last time.

PROPER 6

Sunday between 12 and 18 June inclusive (if after Trinity Sunday)

How we welcome people into the church is important, and should teach us about how we welcome God into our lives.

1 Kings 21.1b–10 (11–14) 15–21a
Galatians 2.15–21
Luke 7.36—8.3

- Designated group leaders.
- Speakers.

□ *Starter*

Explore how we make people feel welcome in a variety of situations. The week before the service appoint a number of group leaders and allocate the groupwork below. This will allow them to prepare for the discussion, and to bring in a suitable speaker for their group.

During the service divide the congregation into mixed-age groups (or alternatively allocate suitable subjects to some children's groups), with a leader and a speaker. Allow at least 5 to 10 minutes for the groups to explore the subject and listen to their speaker.

Group 1   Look at how a family might welcome a foster child. Invite a foster-parent to come and talk to the group about how they prepare for a child joining the family. Encourage the group to ask questions and make their own suggestions. Is it different with different aged children? What happens when a foster family take on short-term emergency fostering (for example, when a parent suddenly goes into hospital)? Can there be any difficulties?

Group 2   Look at how a school welcomes reception children or new children joining another year in the school. Invite a reception teacher to come and talk about how they welcome children into the school. Do they involve other children, or work with parents before the children join the school? Do things ever go wrong?

Group 3   Look at how a new baby is welcomed into the family. Invite some new parents and their baby to talk about how they welcomed the baby. What preparations did they make? What did people buy for the baby? How did older children welcome the baby? What kind of welcome did the baby get from grandparents or aunts and uncles? Were there any problems?

Group 4   Look at how an adult is welcomed into the church through baptism. Invite a recently baptized adult (or someone who was baptized as an adult) to come and talk about the welcome they received into the church. What happened when they first went to church? Who spoke to them? Did they feel welcome? Who helped them to learn more about God? Were there any problems?

Group 5   (and as many more groups as necessary) Look at how someone is welcomed into a 'club'. The 'club' might be anything, e.g. the Junior Church, a bowls club, the WI, the Mothers' Union, or the Army. Invite someone from the 'club' to come and talk to the group. How do they welcome new members? Is there some sort of welcoming ceremony? When can it be said that someone has actually 'joined'? How much thought goes into welcoming new people? Are there ever any problems?

☐   *Optional*

One group could look at how a baby, rather than an adult, is welcomed into the church through baptism.

☐   *Comment*

In the reading from St Luke's Gospel we see Simon the Pharisee welcoming Jesus into his house for a meal. Or rather, we see Simon the man of good birth and even better social standing not really welcoming Jesus into his house.

As a Pharisee Simon lived by the precepts of the Law of Moses. The Law was all-important to him, and as such Jesus put him in a difficult situation, for here was a man who was unclean. Jesus consorted with sinners and outcasts, and this made him ritually unclean. For such a man to enter the house of a Pharisee was to make the house and everyone else unclean. But Simon is so intrigued by Jesus he overlooks these faults, and actually sits down to eat with him.

However, despite his interest Simon does not give Jesus the outward signs of welcome any Jew might have expected. He does not give him the kiss of welcome, nor does he offer water to wash his feet or a towel to dry them, nor does he anoint his head. It is the Samaritan woman who follows Jesus and in washing his feet with her tears, and drying them with her hair, does all this. Great though her sin is, it is she who welcomes Jesus and it is she who is forgiven.

We have learnt something about welcoming people today. But we have also learnt something about welcoming God into our lives. The truest welcome comes from the heart, and just as other people know when they are really welcome, so God knows when we really want him in our lives.

☐ *Conclusion*

Look at how the congregation welcome new people into church. Use a flip-chart or an OHP and list what actually happens under two headings: Positive and Negative. Be brave, and listen to the comments of any newcomer or visitor.

Take the results away and report them to the PCC or church council. Set up a working party to make changes, if necessary.

PROPER 7

Sunday between 19 and 25 June inclusive (if after Trinity Sunday)

On our journey of life, even when we feel we have reached a dead end, or are going the wrong way, like Elijah we can discover God is there ready to restore our faith.

1 Kings 19.1–4 (5–7), 8–15a
Galatians 3.23–29
Luke 8.26–39

- One or more large mazes and people to prepare them.
- Optional: A4 photocopies of the maze.
- Pencils.
- A4 sheets of paper for the time-lines.
- Pencils.

☐ *Starter*

Create the most complicated maze possible, see page 99. Use a blackboard laid flat on a table, a very large sheet of paper, or frieze paper. It would probably be advisable to create a draft maze first

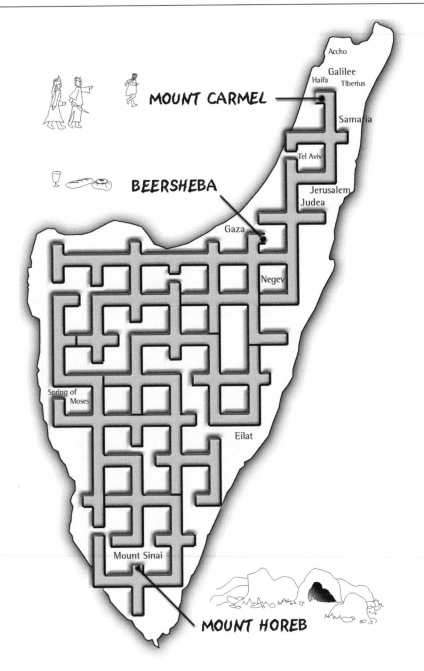

MOUNT CARMEL

BEERSHEBA

MOUNT HOREB

before transferring it to the larger paper. If the congregation is very large you might need to create two or three big mazes, or make photocopies for everyone.

Remind the congregation of the story they have just heard. Elijah is fleeing King Ahab and Queen Jezebel after the battle with the prophets of Baal. First he flees to the safety of the desert, near Beersheba. Here he lays down completely exhausted and wishing he were dead. But God has other plans for him and he receives nourishment from an angel who instructs him to 'eat' before travelling to Mount Horeb (i.e. Mount Sinai, probably somewhere in the middle of the Sinai peninsular) where God awaits him.

The task for the congregation is to follow the path that Elijah took as he fled from the king, and to find his first refuge. Then they are to follow his path to Mount Horeb until they find the cave.

□ *Comment*

The amazing contest with the prophets of Baal is only just over. Elijah has demonstrated the awesome power of Yahweh (God), the people have confessed their faith, and the prophets of Baal have been slain. At this point we might have thought the contest was over, but in the very next scene we see Elijah fleeing the wrath of King Ahab and Queen Jezebel. Baalism has certainly not ended, even if it has suffered a temporary setback.

Elijah flees south from the territory of King Ahab, whose headquarters are based in Samaria. He heads south into the wilderness of southern Judah, and a day's journey south of Beersheba. A broken, despairing man, he throws himself under the shade of a juniper tree (or 'broom' tree in some translations). How has he been any better than others, he asks himself? In attempting to destroy the idolatry all around him, he too has resorted to violence. He must also have wondered if God was so supreme why was it that Jezebel was still able to exert such influence?

It is at this point, lonely and dejected, he wishes he were dead. But in his darkest hour he discovers Yahweh has not deserted him. An angel (or a passing Bedouin?) ministers to him, giving him a cake and a jar of water. But Elijah is still too depressed to bother to eat. It takes a second visit from the angel to prompt him into eating, and to give him a message. He is to continue on his journey.

Forty days later (the traditional time to signify a long journey in the Old Testament), Elijah comes to Mount Horeb and finds a cave in which to lodge. It is here that he is visited by God, and gives the most wonderful reply. God asks, 'What you doing here?' and Elijah answers, 'I have been very zealous for the Lord . . . and they are seeking my life, to take it away' (1 Kings 19.9–10). Like a small child he doesn't answer God, but makes excuses for his actions.

Nevertheless it is here that Elijah's faith is restored. Like Moses before him God demonstrates his power, though unlike Moses, God is not in the earthquake, the wind or the fire. He is heard in the lull that follows all three. He is heard in the awesome silence left behind after these events.

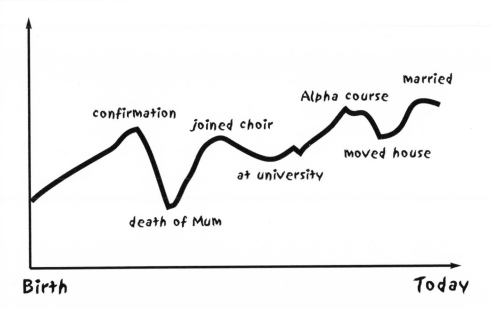

As we saw in our maze, the journey of life isn't very easy. We get disheartened and stuck in dead ends as Elijah did with his demonstration against the prophets of Baal; we get lost as he did when he gave up under the tree at Beersheba, and we don't know which way to go; sometimes we feel God is very far away as Elijah did, and like him we give up; but even at our lowest point when we think we are totally alone and lost on our journey we can find a refuge like Elijah's cave and discover God is already there.

For the modern Christian the dead-ends and the feeling of being lost can come when we forget to pray and read our Bibles. Then we need to return to the path through prayer, to continue the journey once more, in the knowledge that he will restore our faith.
(from an idea by Judy Jones)

 ☐ *Conclusion*

Give out sheets of paper and pencils and ask everyone to draw a time-line showing the times in their life when their faith has been strong, and times when their faith has been weak. Where are they now on this time-line? Encourage adults and children to work together.

Allow some time of silent prayer at the end of this part of the service.

PROPER 8

Sunday between 26 June and 2 July inclusive

What does it mean to say that we follow someone? What does it mean to say that we are followers of Jesus, or to be asked to follow Jesus?

2 Kings 2.1–2, 6–14
Galatians 5.1, 13–25
Luke 9.51–62

- Bibles.
- Group leaders.
- The Disciples worksheets.
- Pens or pencils.
- Optional: Art materials for children's group.

□ *Starter*

Invite some adults and children to 'follow' you, or invite all the congregation to follow you. Take those who follow on some kind of obstacle course, inside or outside the church. Make it as difficult as possible. For example: Walk along a row of suitably chosen people so that you have to climb over or round their legs, or climb over an obstacle, or crawl under something.

Finally stop and discuss the activity with the group:

- What did it feel like?
- What was bad about it?
- What was good about it?

□ *Optional*

If the whole congregation followed, discuss with any who were unable to walk (perhaps the elderly) what it felt like to be left behind.

Divide the congregation into small groups, keeping any children in one or more separate groups. Allocate group leaders and give each group some Bibles, and a copy of 'The Disciples' worksheet on page 103.

The children's group should look at examples of the disciples following Jesus (Matthew 4.18–22; Luke 9.1–6, etc.), and of their difficulties (Mark 4.35–41; Luke 22.39–46, etc.). Tell the stories

* THE DISCIPLES *

Think of examples that show the disciples as 'followers' of Jesus

Think of examples that show the disciples had difficulties following Jesus

As a group, what do you find most difficult about following Jesus?

using a children's Bible and allow the group to express these examples in painting or collage work.

☐ *Conclusion*

Gather the whole congregation together and look at some of the information discovered. You could also look at some of the difficulties the present-day Christian finds in following Christ.

☐ *Comment*

St Luke sees life as a long journey. The early part of his Gospel is full of journeys: Mary travels to see her cousin Elizabeth; Mary and Joseph travel to Bethlehem; and the holy family travel to Jerusalem to present Jesus at the Temple. In his own life Luke also travels. He accompanies Paul around the Mediterranean. But behind all this lies the story of the other great journey – the 40 years of travelling in the desert by the whole Jewish nation.

The one thing such a seasoned traveller knew was that journeys had their ups and downs. Life was not always easy, and the path might indeed prove to be very difficult, or indeed might fail to take the traveller to the place required. Anything might happen on a journey in the Roman empire, shipwreck or attack by bandits included.

Following Jesus is rather like one of these journeys. It doesn't mean life will be easy. Sometimes there will be difficulties and we will lose our way. At other times things will be plain sailing. But whatever the journey is like, our task is to keep on following Jesus through thick and thin.

PROPER 9

Sunday between 3 and 9 July inclusive

St Paul reminds us we reap what we sow. If we sow evil, we shall reap what is evil; while if we sow what is good, we shall reap eternal life.

2 Kings 5.1–14
Galatians 6.(1–6) 7–16
Luke 10.1–11, 16–20

- Worksheets for all the congregation.
- Alternatively, seeds, plants, flowers or branches.
- Pencils or pens.
- Copies of church policies.
- Copies of PCC or church council agendas for the past year, cut into strips.
- Large sheets of card.

Produce sufficient worksheets based on the example on page 106 for all the congregation.

Alternatively, provide a large variety of seeds, and plants or branches to match them. Encourage the congregation to match the seeds to the plants. Or you could offer flowers to be matched to leaves and branches.

☐ *Comment*

As we have seen it is not always easy to find which seed and which plant go together, never mind trying to identify which plant is which. We would need to be an expert biologist to get it right each time. However, whether or not we knew which seed went with which plant, we would expect a fir cone to produce a fir tree if we grew the seed. We wouldn't expect a tuber to produce a dandelion, or a conker to produce a palm tree. Certain seeds produce certain plants, and that's the law of nature.

Just as in nature, so it is with humans. Those who 'sow' evil in their life will 'reap' the rewards of evil. Those who are concerned only with the joys of this world cannot expect to be rewarded by their heavenly Father at the end of their lives. Those who ignore the plight of the sick, and the suffering in this world, cannot expect anything in the next world.

As Christians, both as individuals and as the church, we are called to sow all that is good, to work for the benefit of others, and to love our neighbour as ourselves. We are never to give up living the life Jesus taught us, no matter how difficult this way might be. Our reward will be to reap what we sow, and to gain eternal life.

☐ *Conclusion*

Look at your church's policies, and explore what the church might expect to reap from them. One way of doing this might be, prior to the service, to make a copy of one year's worth of church council agendas. Cut these up into different agenda subjects, e.g. 'Church Fete', 'Christmas Services', etc. Give out all the slips of paper to the congregation. It doesn't matter if there are too many or too few for the congregation.

Invite the first person to stand up and read what is on their slip,

~ *Plants and their Seeds* ~

Match the seeds to the plants below, by drawing
lines between them.

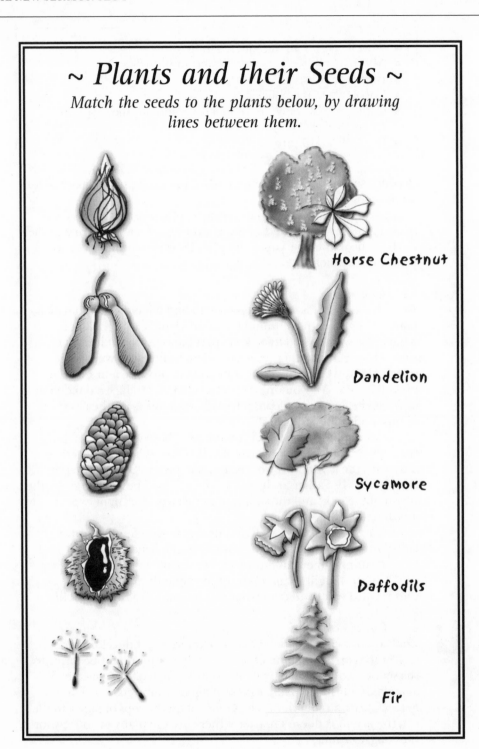

Horse Chestnut

Dandelion

Sycamore

Daffodils

Fir

e.g. 'Churchyard Maintenance'. Ask them to write the subject 'Churchyard Maintenance' onto a fairly large sheet of card and stand out front. Continue until all the slips of paper have been read. Those with duplicate subjects should stand together, and need not make a new subject card.

Finally look at which subjects have come up the most and which the least. What does this say about the sowing and reaping in your church? For example, if Mission has been high on the agenda we might expect the appearance of new Christians would be the result, or that existing Christians would continue to show signs of growth. Has this happened? If churchyard maintenance has been high on the agenda we might expect a well-maintained building, but are there any new people coming into church, and is the nurture of those present adequate?

Resolve to make changes to the church council priorities and agendas, as necessary.

PROPER 10

Sunday between 10 and 16 July inclusive

Who is my neighbour? Is my neighbour only someone who lives next door to me? Can my neighbour be someone I do not know, or whom I might, in fact, dislike? This week's theme allows the congregation to explore such questions.

Amos 7.7–17
Colossians 1.1–14
Luke 10.25–37

- A sheet of paper for each group and a pen or pencil.
- A few current newspapers.
- Paper.
- Felt-tip pens.
- Glue sticks.
- Scissors.
- Copies of the finger puppet instructions.
- Rubber bands.

□ *Starter*

Divide into small mixed-age groups. You might need group enablers. Explore in a concrete fashion the question 'Who is my neighbour?' The group or individuals will need to decide whether this means only those who live either side of or opposite their house, or whether it means all the members in the street or in the block of flats. One way of deciding might be to see how many people each person can name. Write all the names down on a sheet of paper. Keep this to form the basis of a prayer list for the group.

Now look again much more widely at the question of 'Who is my neighbour?'

● Who else might the group want to include?
● Are there any the group would not want to include?

At this point hear back very briefly from the groups, to allow everyone to listen to some of the results so far.

□ *Comment*

Jesus told the story of the Good Samaritan to a man who was a lawyer, and the lawyer we are told was trying to trap Jesus. Perhaps he was a young man trying to make a name for himself, we don't know. But what we do know is that the lawyer asked Jesus, 'What must I do to inherit eternal life?' We could put it another way and ask, 'How do I get to heaven?' or 'How can I be saved?'

Jesus replies with a very traditional answer straight from the scriptures. He says, 'You shall love the Lord your God with all your heart, and with all your soul, and with all your strength, and with all your mind; and your neighbour as yourself.' Only then as a good Jewish man, obeying the Law of Moses, will he be accepted by God. But this is not enough for the man and he asks, 'And who is my neighbour?'

Jesus answers him by telling the parable of the Good Samaritan, which effectively says that your neighbour is the very last person in the world you might imagine. All good Jews loathed their neighbours the Samaritans, for they had set up a rival temple and gone their own way. But Jesus tells the man this is the very person who is his neighbour. This is exactly the person he should love, like himself. Only then will he be obeying God's Law.

□ *Conclusion*

Give everyone in the congregation sufficient materials to make a finger puppet. Also give them (or put up somewhere) copies of some ideas, as on page 109. Adults and children may work alone or together. The only instruction is they should make a finger puppet of someone (which could be an individual, or someone from a specific nation) they dislike. This person should be the one person in

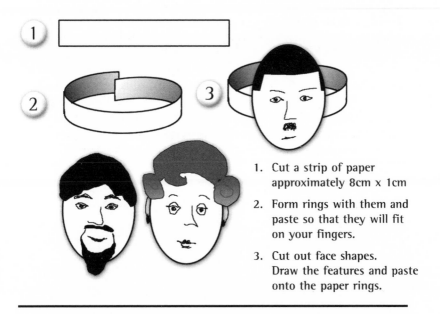

1. Cut a strip of paper approximately 8cm x 1cm
2. Form rings with them and paste so that they will fit on your fingers.
3. Cut out face shapes. Draw the features and paste onto the paper rings.

the world they would find most difficult to love. Should anyone find this impossible, a quick reminder of the news might help – which country is oppressing another; which person has been recently convicted of a horrific crime?

Try making the finger puppets in silence if possible, spending the time thinking about the person you are depicting. This is the very person God says you should love in the way you love yourself.

Finally, when most of the finger puppets are completed close this part of the service with the following prayer, as everyone looks at their own particular 'neighbour':

Lord God,
Help us to see that all people are our neighbours,
even those whom we find most difficult to love.
Help us to learn to love all people,
and especially those of whom we have been thinking.
Amen.

PROPER 11

Sunday between 17 and 23 July inclusive

God sometimes calls us to lay aside our worldly concerns and to concentrate on the things of the Spirit. We need to learn when one is more important than the other.

Amos 8.1–12
Colossians 1.15–28
Luke 10.38–42

- The Dramatized Bible.
- Bibles.
- 2 people to act as Martha and Mary.
- Collage paper and materials.
- Glue.

☐ *Starter*

Tell the Gospel story using the Dramatized Bible. The week before the service appoint two characters to be 'Martha' and 'Mary'. These may or may not be those who will take part in the Gospel reading for the day. Their task, with the leader of the service, is to study the Gospel story and to prepare answers for possible questions.

Divide the congregation into small mixed-age groups of up to 8–10 people. Include older children, but gather younger children into their own group with an adult leader. Give each group a copy of the Gospel story, or sufficient copies of the Bible for everyone, and allocate the character of Martha or Mary to each group. Also give each group a copy of the questions below.

In the groups re-read the story, looking at it particularly from the aspect of the character allocated to the group. Then spend some time discussing the story, asking these questions:

- What kind of a person does this character seem to be? (e.g. lively, kind, thoughtful, etc.)
- How might she have felt at the start of the story?
- How might she have felt about the other two characters in the story?
- What might she have liked to say to either of the other two characters in the story?

□ *Conclusion*

After sufficient time has been allowed in order to reach some conclusions about the two characters, ask each group to produce one or two questions they would like to ask Martha or Mary. When this has been done, put the two people chosen the previous week in the 'hot seat', and invite groups to ask their questions of Martha and Mary.

Groups with young children might like to explore the Gospel story in a different manner, by looking at the two different kinds of characters portrayed by Martha and Mary. Look at how people are very different: some are active and some less so; some like to listen to stories, some like to draw or paint, etc. Finally, make a large collage of the story, using all sorts of scraps of material to complete the picture. The work should be prepared in outline beforehand.

□ *Optional*

Alternatively, send two people from each group representing Mary to a group representing Martha and vice versa. Allow the groups to ask questions of the visitors, and hear possible answers. By sending two Marthas and two Marys, it will be easier for them to think up answers.

□ *Comment*

The story of Martha and Mary teaches us so much about right attitudes to God and to other people. It comes at the end of a section of Luke's Gospel dealing to some extent with hospitality, after the sending out of the 70, and the parable of the Good Samaritan. The Christian is to welcome the opportunity to serve and to give.

But the story also shows us something of the hidden life of this family. Martha and Mary have presumably lived together for many years, so much of their character will be known to the other. It can be no surprise to Martha that Mary wishes to listen to Jesus rather than to work. Yet she involves the guests in bringing into the open her complaint against her sister. This is not the loving action of a good host.

Jesus does not, it must be noticed, say that Martha's desire to work for her guests is wrong. Indeed, to be a good host is desirable. But in this instance he acknowledges Mary has chosen the 'better part'. The concern with the things of this world is once again contrasted with the things of God. The arrival of a teacher in the household should mean all would want to listen and learn at his feet, but Martha we are told is 'worried and distracted by many things'.

We need to learn when to be practical and when to put aside our daily activities in favour of learning more about God and our faith. There is a time and a place for both.

PROPER 12

Sunday between 24 and 30 July inclusive

This week explores the words of The Lord's Prayer in greater depth through a variety of means.

Hosea 1.2–10
Colossians 2.6–15 (16–19)
Luke 11.1–13

- Words of the Lord's Prayer.
- Slips of paper with one line of the Lord's Prayer on them.
- Newspapers and magazines.
- Bibles.
- Hymn books (modern and older versions).
- Scissors.
- Art and craft materials.
- Collage material.
- Large sheets of paper, or frieze paper.
- Free trade information and leaflets.

□ *Starter*

The week before the service appoint group leaders and allocate them one line of the Lord's Prayer. Preferably use the 'new' version of the Lord's Prayer. Their task is to furnish materials needed for each group to explore their particular line of the Lord's Prayer, through art, craft, drama, or any other suitable media. The leaders are to provide materials, but should allow their group to come up with ideas within the media chosen. Here are some examples that might be used, but others will be just as suitable:

- **Our Father in heaven**: Explore the notion of the Good Father by looking at examples from newspapers or magazines or look up images of God in the Bible (New and/or Old Testament) which show evidence of God as a Good Father (or find parables or stories in the Bible of good fathers). Create a collage based on your discoveries. Alternatively, as a group, create a story about a good father.
- **Hallowed be your name**: Discuss the meaning of 'hallowed'; look up Isaiah's calling and his vision of God in Isaiah 6; explore how it might be possible to 'hallow' God's name today; find as

many names for God as possible and then look up their meanings; look at some famous hymns or psalms and decide what they say about God's name. Produce some artwork based on the different names for God.

- **Your kingdom come**: Look up and read different kingdom parables (e.g. the leaven (Matthew 13.33); the great treasure (Matthew 13.44); the pearl of great price (Matthew 13.45); the net (Matthew 13.47–50), etc.). What do these tell you about the kingdom of God? What characteristics might epitomize God's kingdom? Jesus says that God's kingdom is both here and is to come. How might this be? Create one or two static 'photographs' (i.e. tableaux) showing what God's kingdom on earth might be like. This could be combined with a tableau showing what God's kingdom is not like (e.g. clenched fists and a fight for the latter, and a loving and caring image for the former).

- **Your will be done**: Talk about free will. What does it mean exactly? What might God's will be? What might he want for his people? How much does free will lie behind some of the world's disasters (e.g. flooding caused by deforestation, etc.)? Explore newspapers or magazines to find evidence. Finally look for examples that show free will can lead to something good happening. Create a collage out of these articles with a suitable heading.

- **On earth as in heaven**: Talk about free will. What does it mean exactly? What might God's will be? Look up some of the following readings and explore the notion of God's idea of free will, and what he expects of us:
  - Adam and Eve (Genesis 3.1–7 [or 1–13]).
  - The wickedness of people (Genesis 6.5–8).
  - The people of Sodom (Genesis 18.20–33).
  - The call of the disciples (Mark 1.16–20).
  - The rich young ruler (Luke 18.18–27).
  - Peter denies Jesus (Luke 22.31–34; 22.39–46; 22.54–62).
  Make one personal 'promise to God' (rather like a New Year's resolution) concerned with your faith. If desired write all of them up onto a large sheet of paper and hang up in the church.

- **Give us today our daily bread**: Hold a discussion about the food we eat – what is essential, what is junk food, can we be more responsible in our buying and eating; make a list of all the food eaten by the group over the past 24 hours; look at the Fair Trade situation with the help of materials from Oxfam or Christian Aid and find out whether individuals or the church as a whole can do anything to help; create a simple poster to represent some of your thinking.

- **And forgive us our sins**: Before the service make a list of the seven deadly sins on a large sheet of paper, then look at them as a group making sure everyone understands their meaning. Take another large sheet of paper and brainstorm every sin of which the group can think, e.g. kidnapping, anonymous letter, slander, etc. The group could use magazines and newspapers to help, if desired. Finally, look at the list and decide which two cause individuals the most difficulty, and as a group which two cause our country and the world the most difficulties. As a group ask God's forgiveness.

- **As we forgive those who sin against us**: As a group discuss the following: 'We are a nation who need to blame someone when things go wrong, how could this be changed?' If possible come up with some concrete examples of how changes could be made, and list on a large sheet. Alternatively produce some role-play of a situation that leads to the need to blame someone (e.g. a hospital tragedy).

- **Lead us not into temptation**: Create a top-ten list of temptations (e.g. eating sweets, gossiping, staying in bed, etc.) as a group. Having created the list, add no. 11 and leave it empty. Then, individually, allocate each item on the list a number from 1–10 (no. 10 being the most tempting). No. 11 can be used to add any personal temptation not on the list. Share with your neighbour what causes you the most difficulty.

- **But deliver us from evil**: Using the phrase 'Evil is . . .' come up with a list of what evil means to the group. You might want to use newspapers to help create the definition. Optionally, find out what evil would have meant to Jesus and his disciples by looking at Matthew 4.1–11; Mark 1. 21–26; Luke 10.17–20; Luke 11.14–20; Matthew 7.9–11; and Matthew 25.31–46 (or 41–46). Compare with what you would consider to be evil in today's world. Write your conclusions up on a large sheet of paper.

- **For the kingdom, the power, and the glory are yours, now and for ever. Amen**: Discuss the meaning of this phrase. The following Bible readings might help: Matthew 13.31–33; 13.44–46; Matthew 8.23–27; Acts 3.1–8; Isaiah 6.1–6; Revelation 4. Create some artwork to reflect your thinking.

 ☐ *Note*

The text of the Lord's Prayer above reflects Matthew's version as found in Matthew 6.9–13, and is the text customarily used in worship.

 ☐ *Comment*

Jesus teaches his disciples by example, whether it is through praying, story-telling, or healing, and the disciples strive to follow what he has shown them. So it is interesting to note that when the disciples come to ask Jesus about prayer, he is actually praying:

> He was praying in a certain place, and after he had finished, one of his disciples said to him, 'Lord, teach us to pray . . .' (Luke 11.1)

This is no textbook technique that is taught. Jesus teaches his disciples out of his intimate knowledge of what it means to speak to the Father. He does not wrap up the words in pretty language (as we so often do), but addresses God as 'Father'. He uses the diminutive form 'Abba', unlike Matthew who is more formal (see Matthew 6.9). As adoptive sons and daughters we too can have this close and intimate relationship with God.

The first petitions in the Lord's Prayer are concerned with God and his kingdom: 'Hallowed be your name', 'Your kingdom come' and 'Your will be done'. Is this not how we too should pray, first to be aware of God's majesty and glory and of his work in our world, before the petitions become more personal?

The second petitions concern themselves with our needs: 'Give us today our daily bread', 'And forgive us our sins as we forgive those who sin against us', 'Lead us not into temptation', and 'But deliver us from evil'. Although we say these words frequently, they pack a huge punch. All too often we automatically say, 'And forgive us our sins as we forgive those who sin against us', yet our world shows evidence that this is usually forgotten in the desire for retribution and vengeance. The 'Give us today our daily bread' is all too often exclusive, and we forget those who have no daily bread.

The final section of the Lord's Prayer returns to God's concerns, reflecting that all our prayers should start and end with God's concerns, for the kingdom, the power and the glory are, as we say, his!

 ☐ *Conclusion*
Share results with one another, display artwork, and watch role-play as appropriate.

PROPER 13

Sunday between 31 July and 6 August inclusive

Jesus teaches it is wrong to be concerned only with the things of this world. Materialism, in whatever shape it takes, is a danger to the Christian and is of no lasting value.

Hosea 11.1–11
Colossians 3.1–11
Luke 12.13–21

☐ *Note*

This week could be used in conjunction with the following week.

- Labels.
- List of things important to the world.
- Felt-tip pens.
- Helpers.
- Large sheets of paper.
- Prit-tak or drawing pins.
- Fat felt-tip pens.

☐ *Starter*

Before the service create a large number of sticky labels. Each should have a word that describes something 'the world' thinks is important, see the list below.

☐ *Optional*

Draw pictures to describe the words below.

Important to the world

Gold	Jewels
Silver	Car
Money	Holiday
Cheque book	Computer
House	Toys
Cottage	Clothes
Bank account	Sports
Home	Gardening
Music	Arts
University	Work

There can be duplicate words, and the list above is far from exhaustive. Appoint a number of helpers, and get them to stick a label onto everyone's back. Make sure no-one has any idea what their word or picture says.

Now instruct everyone to discover what their own word says by questioning others. They may ask only one question:

- Can you describe what my word says?

Encourage everyone to describe the word without using it (e.g. jewels: 'worn by men and women'), and allocate suitable words to children (e.g. 'toys', 'computer', 'money', or 'clothes').

You may need to have some spare words for those people who discover their word almost immediately. Invite them to have a second or even a third attempt. Finally, when most people have discovered their word ask them to sit down.

☐ *Comment*

The story of the Rich Fool in St Luke's Gospel seems to have been taken from some words in Ecclesiasticus 11.18–20:

> One becomes rich through diligence and self-denial,
> and the reward allotted to him is this:
> when he says, 'I have found rest,
> and now I shall feast on my goods!'
> he does not know how long it will be
> until he leaves them to others and dies.

With a few carefully chosen words Luke give us a vivid picture of the man who puts all his trust in his work and his wealth. Ultimately these are of no value, for when God demands his soul at death, he can take none of his goods with him. As the verse from Ecclesiasticus reminds us, at our death all our belongings are left to someone else.

As if to emphasize the man's character the parable is full of self, the words 'I' and 'my' are used 11 times, e.g.:

> I will do this: I will pull down my barns and build larger ones,
> and there I will store all my grain and my goods.

The rich fool is so taken up with himself and his wealth that he does not see there are other things more important in life. While he concentrates on the material things of this life, he has ignored the things that really matter; while he builds larger barns and stores his crops, he has forgotten to concentrate on his spiritual life.

Jesus is not saying it is wrong to work hard and to save, indeed it would be wrong to be lazy or squander what we do have, but he is saying it is wrong to put all our emphasis on the things of this world. We should not be overly concerned with the material things of life – with our home, our work, or our hobbies – for ultimately these are not important to God. Indeed many of the things of this world distract us from doing what God wants us to do.

□ *Conclusion*

Divide into small groups and look at some of the 'word labels'. How can these be used in a negative and in a positive way? For example:

'Money'   can be saved and never spent, or can be spent on selfish
               things
               can be used to help others
'Home'   can be an inward, self-contained, private place
               can be outward looking, and welcoming to others

Be as honest as possible and try to decide when something is inherently wrong. Even love of one's family can become idolatrous when it becomes more important than God! Be sure to include things the children will understand.

If desired, hold a plenary session and report back conclusions. Alternatively write up the words on large sheets of paper, with a summary of the good and bad ways they can be used. Place these around the church and allow people to look at them later.

Include prayers for the right use of resources and possessions in the Intercessions.

PROPER 14

Sunday between 7 and 13 August inclusive

This week continues the theme that things of this world have no permanent value. Only the things of God are permanent.

Isaiah 1.1, 10–20
Hebrews 11.1–3, 8–16
Luke 12.32–40

□ *Note*

This week could be used in conjunction with last week.

- Multiple copies of the texts for hiding around the church.
- Bibles for every group.
- Large sheets of paper and fat felt-tip pens for every group.
- Prit-tak or drawing pins.
- Copies of the Text of the Week card for everyone.
- Pens or pencils for everyone.

☐ *Starter*

Create a treasure trail around the church and its environment. Seek to make the trail as physically wide as possible and include many more texts than can be found. Hide the texts in every conceivable place where children and adults might look. Each text will need to have multiple copies to allow one for each group, e.g. 50 copies of each text if there are 50 groups or pairs. Here are some suggestions of texts that might be used, but these are by no means exhaustive, and if the congregation is large more might be needed:

Matthew 5.5	Matthew 5.6
Matthew 5.7	Matthew 5.8
Matthew 5.9	Matthew 5.11
Matthew 5.13	Matthew 5.14
Matthew 5.15	Matthew 5.16
Matthew 5.41	Matthew 5.42
Matthew 5.43–45a	Matthew 6.6
Matthew 6.14	Matthew 6.17–18
Matthew 6.19–20	Matthew 6.22–23
Matthew 6.24b	Matthew 6.25
Matthew 6.28–29	Matthew 6.30
Matthew 6.31, 33	Matthew 7.1
Matthew 7.3	Matthew 7.12
Matthew 7.13–14	Matthew 7.18–19
Matthew 7.24–25	Mark 3.29–30
Mark 3.35	Mark 4.24b
Mark 8.38	Mark 9.35b
Mark 9.36–37	Mark 9.40
Mark 9.42	Mark 9.43–44
Mark 9.45–46	Mark 9.47
Mark 10.14b	Mark 10.15
Luke 12.33a	Luke 12.33b
Luke 12.34	Luke 13.6–9
Luke 13.23–24	Luke 16.10
Luke 16.13b	John 3.5
John 3.16	John 3.18
John 4.48	John 6.27

John 6.35	John 6.47
John 6.48	John 6.51
John 6.54	John 6.56
John 6.63	

Allow the congregation to work in small groups, as they prefer. These might be families, or simply pairs. Should there be those who cannot easily move from their seats encourage a group to come back to this person each time a text is found. Each group should have access to a modern Bible of any version.

The task of each group is to find a text. Groups should be encouraged to start in entirely different directions, to avoid a 'traffic jam'. When texts are found they should be taken away from the scene (perhaps back to the group's original seats), looked up in the Bible, and read. This will also ensure that other groups don't necessarily see where the clue was hidden, and will keep the 'hunt' element going for longer.

At the outset explain that should they find something like '33a', or '33b', the 'a' means the first half of the verse, and 'b' the second half of a verse.

After some time (depending on what time you have available), when the groups have found a fair number of texts, call 'time', and invite the groups to return to their seats.

Text of the Week

□ *Comment*

Jesus emphasizes it is important to concentrate on the things that last. If we buy a car we expect to be able to drive it for some time, we don't expect it to fail after a few months. Ordinary common sense leads us to buy things in our daily life that will last, and this is just the point Jesus is making.

Possessions can be a disadvantage, because they can get in the way of the things that really matter. If we spend all our time concentrating on the things of the world (working, learning to play golf, etc.) then we shall neglect the things God thinks are important. By putting all our time and effort into the things of the world, we are actually putting our time and effort into something that won't last.

The texts we have been looking up remind us that God's priorities are different from the world's. Only when we concentrate on his priorities will we be investing in something that lasts eternally.

□ *Conclusions*

Each group should now make a list of how God wants us to live and of the characteristics he wants us to acquire, based on the texts they have found. Write these up onto large sheets of paper, using a fat felt-tip pen.

Obviously many of these lists will be duplicates, but place as many as possible up on the walls of the church or hall, and leave for a week or two.

Finally, photocopy the example of the Text of the Week card on page 120 and give to all the congregation. Encourage them to write one of the texts onto the card and to use this in private prayer over the coming week.

PROPER 15

Sunday between 14 and 20 August inclusive

A deeper look at the Old Testament reading for the day reminds us that God has the right to destroy his own creation if it fails to produce the fruit expected.

Isaiah 5.1–7
Hebrews 11.29—12.2
Luke 12.49–56

- Bibles or copies of the Isaiah reading for everyone.
- Workshop leaders.
- OHP or flip-chart and fat felt-tip pen.
- Music for the mime group.
- Choral speaking 'framework'.
- Art materials, e.g. paper, brushes, paint, etc.

□ *Starter*

Before the service organize a number of workshop leaders to run different groups:

- Mime.
- Dance.
- Drama.
- Choral speaking.
- Artwork.

Put up the group names on an OHP or flip-chart so that all the congregation can see them.

Allow the congregation time to decide how they wish to explore the Old Testament reading: in mime, dance, drama, speech, or artwork. Some people might choose to work in pairs, depending on the medium of their choice.

Encourage *every group* to start by reading Isaiah 5.1–7 through at least twice, before placing the Bibles out of sight and relying on their memory. The following are suggestions as to how groups might explore the 'Vineyard Song':

□ *Workshops*

1 Mime

As a group create some mime to accompany a reading of the song. Take particular care to notice the change from 'my beloved' (verse 1) to 'and now inhabitants of Jerusalem . . . judge between me' (verse 3), and 'what I will do to my vineyard' (verse 5). Encourage the group to work out their own movements and to use their memories as much as possible. The leader should do some thinking about the piece before the service, but should allow the group to lead as much as possible.

2 Dance

Before the service the leader will need to choose some music to accompany this item, and will need to find somewhere to work away from other groups. Encourage the group to create their own movements as much as possible. Start by creating a list of the basic events of the story, from memory. Check these for accuracy before creating movement. Keep the movement suitable for all ages, and for men and women.

3 Drama

Keep this group distinctly different from the Mime group. The leader should prepare beforehand, but allow direction as to the final scenario from the group. If possible this group should be fairly large, allowing for the following characters:

- Inhabitants of Jerusalem (or the judge).
- People of Judah (or the judge).
- Narrator (or the barrister).
- My beloved (or the litigant).
- Vines (or the defendants).

Establish the order of the story and allow characters to work on making up their own lines. The story could be told as though in a courtroom. Keep the movement and the language short and pithy.

4 Choral speaking

Before the service the leader might like to prepare for this workshop, though they should leave the group to come up with actual words. A framework like the following might help the group get started:

What happened
(Who?) i.e. God (or my beloved)
(What?) i.e. had a vineyard
(Where?) i.e. on a sunny hill
(What then?) i.e. he dug and planted
(What?) i.e. vines
(What then?)

Judge between me
(What?)
(What?)
(Why?)

What I shall do now
(What?)
(What?)
(What?)
(Who?)

Having put in the basic blocks of information, get the group to play with the words, interjecting *short, sharp, exclamations*, or inserting echo sounds, or queries. When the group are happy with the words, get them to prepare it as a piece of choral verse speaking.

5 Artwork

Invite this group to identify the basic parts of the story in say six or seven sections, e.g. the planting, the watch-tower, the first yield, etc.

Divide the group and allocate different scenes. Draw outline pictures of these scenes on very large sheets of paper, keeping the drawings bold and non-fussy. If desired paint these pictures, or create collage work. Give each picture a title. They could accompany the mime or drama groups' work, if time permits.

☐ *Conclusion*

Watch as many of the finished productions as possible. Any group who chooses not to show their work (perhaps because it is not finished) may opt out.

☐ *Comment*

Isaiah invites his audience to listen to a story about the owner of a vineyard. He calls them to sympathize and even to act as judges; to vindicate the owner's action in rooting out and destroying his vines. Despite everything he has done in preparing the ground, and in protecting and nurturing his vines, all that grows is wild grapes. He had expected luscious grapes fit for wine-making, but all that grows are the small, sour wild grapes.

What more could the vineyard owner do? It was time to cut his losses and pull out, to take down the hedge, remove the wall, and allow the wild plants to overgrow the area once more. As the owner of the vineyard, was it not his right to destroy what he had created?

Just as Isaiah's listeners are in agreement with him about the justification of the vineyard owner to destroy his work, he changes his tune, and it becomes apparent the vineyard is the house of Israel, and the vines are the people of Judah. Despite all God's care and nurture they have ignored his ways. Instead of justice, God sees bloodshed.

The warning to Isaiah's listeners is clear. But it is also clear to us. We too are God's vines, and we have been planted and nurtured by him. If we ignore his words we too will be uprooted and destroyed.

PROPER 16

Sunday between 21 and 27 August inclusive

An exploration of how various people are commissioned and authorized to undertake their work, together with a fresh look at the commissioning of Jeremiah, reminds us that we too were commissioned at our baptism.

Jeremiah 1.4–10
Hebrews 12.18–29
Luke 13.10–17

> - 4 or 5 speakers.
> - Copies of the Baptism or Confirmation Service (or Admittance to Membership).

□ *Starter*

Explore the way people are commissioned to different jobs. In the week before the service invite people doing any of the following jobs to come and talk about how they were commissioned (or authorized) to do the work. Encourage them to bring any licences or other evidence of their commissioning. Ideally there should be four or five speakers covering a variety of different jobs:

- Priest/minister.
- Deacon.
- Chalice assistant.
- Lay reader.
- Policeman/woman.
- Service man/woman.
- Teacher.
- Scout or Guide leader.

Ask each of those chosen to talk about how they got their job, what training was involved, whether or not there was a formal service of commissioning, and whether or not they have a job description. Restrict each speaker to a few minutes.

□ *Comment*

In our Old Testament reading today we see Jeremiah being commissioned for his work as a prophet. First, he is called by God, who reminds him he has known him since before his birth. From before he was conceived, God had already consecrated him for the work he was to do.

Jeremiah tries to escape his destiny, but God will hear nothing of this. He forestalls Jeremiah's objections by saying he will put his words into the prophet's mouth, and he will be with him at all times. This thought echoes that found in Psalm 139 where God says he is all around us, and there is nowhere we can go to escape his loving hands.

Finally, God touches Jeremiah's tongue and places the words on his lips, before giving him authority over all nations to build them up or to destroy them.

As Christians we too are commissioned and given such authority by virtue of our baptism. As disciples of Christ we are called to nurture others in the faith, to rescue the fallen, help the distressed, seek out the lost, and to take the good news to all people. This is not just the commission given to a priest, a deacon, or a reader. This commission is given to every Christian who truly seeks to carry out his or her ministry as a member of the body of Christ.

 ☐ *Conclusion*

Provide everyone with a copy of the words of the Baptism or Confirmation Service (or Service of Admittance to Membership). In pairs look at what has been promised, explicitly and implicitly by parents and godparents (or adults if the baptism candidate is older) at their commissioning as a Christian. For example, parents promise to bring up children 'to fight against evil and to follow Christ'. Adults also make this promise at their confirmation.

Ask questions like: Have I tried to obey this promise? What has been difficult? What has been easy? Would I say I am gradually maturing as a Christian?

Conclude this part of the service by keeping a moment or two of silence, allowing everyone to make fresh resolutions about their commissioning as a Christian.

PROPER 17

Sunday between 28 August and 3 September inclusive

One of the most difficult lessons to learn for the Christian, is that of humility. True humility is a wonderful characteristic, and one we all need to attain.

Jeremiah 2.4–13
Hebrews 13.1–8, 15–16
Luke 14.1–4, 7–14

- 3 copies of the story.
- 3 people to tell the story: A narrator, a leader, and a landowner.
- 12–25 volunteers.
- Rope or tape for the 'bridge'.

☐ *Starter*

Before the service place two lines of rope or tape in a long line, perhaps down an aisle. The rope should be placed about 25cm apart in parallel lines, with just enough space for someone to stand inside the gap. Ask for 12 volunteers (or up to 25 volunteers) of all ages to stand in a long line, one behind the other, facing the same direction. Appoint two other people, one as the leader of the group and one as the landowner. Give them a copy of the words and invite them to read out their relevant parts. Now tell this story:

A group of friends went on holiday one summer to the beautiful Forest of Maiden. They found a sheltered spot underneath the trees to pitch their tents, and on the second day decided to go for a long walk.

The weather was perfect and they set off in high spirits. The sun shone down through the trees creating a dappled effect, and the birds sang. Nothing could have been more idyllic.

By mid-morning they had reached a large river, the River Maid. Over the years it had cut its way into the soft rock creating a ravine, and the water now lay some 30 metres below them. Ahead lay a rope bridge. It looked solid enough, and although some of the party were a little dubious they started on their way across the bridge.

All had started the trek across the bridge when a man suddenly appeared on the far side of the river. He raised his hand in warning.

Landowner	Where do you think you're going?
Leader	We're crossing the river to the other side.
Landowner	Oh no, you're not! This is my land, and I don't allow any trespassers on my property. You'll have to go back!
Leader	But we've been walking all morning, and it's miles to get back.
Landowner	Too bad! That's not my fault.
Leader	Is there no way we can change your mind?
Landowner	Perhaps there is!
Leader	Anything! We'll do anything.
Landowner	OK! Get yourself into age order, with the youngest at the front. But you're not allowed to leave the bridge, and you're not allowed to speak, or mime to each other.
Leader	So how on earth will we be able to decide who is what age?
Landowner	Each of you will have to decide for yourself whether you are older or younger than the person next to you, and move back or forward accordingly. And you'd better hurry up because I haven't got all day.

Encourage the group of volunteers standing in the long line to get themselves into age order, with the youngest at the front and the oldest at the back. Remind them they are not allowed to speak or to mime in any way, but can only make decisions about their own age and those close to them. Neither can they step off the rope bridge but must stay within the rope lines, and may only move around someone else with negotiation (since none may step off the bridge because they would be killed by the steep drop!) Ensure the congregation give no help whatsoever.

Note that the leaders among this group will find this exercise very difficult as they will be unable to organize the whole group since they cannot step off the rope bridge to see the whole line of people. They will only be able to work with the two or three people on either side of them, and since they cannot mime or communicate in any way with them, this will add to their sense of frustration.

When the task is completed, and the leader is now somewhere in the middle of the group, presuming they are not the youngest, the story continues.

Landowner	Are you now in age order?
Leader	I think so!
Landowner	Well, let us see if that is so. How old are you? (points to the first person) And the next ... and the next ...? (He continues until everyone has given their age. Every time there is a mistake the person should move until they are in the correct place.)
Leader	Can we now cross the bridge, please?

Landowner	Not so fast, you didn't manage to do the last task so well (or 'as you managed the last task so well'), I think I will set another task.
Leader	(groans) We'll be here for ever!
Landowner	(ignoring him) This time, I want you to get yourselves into height order, with the smallest in the front! Oh! The same rules apply!

The group now try again, moving into height order, with the smallest at the front and the tallest at the back. Again there must be no communication between them, or with the congregation.

When this is finished the leader continues.

Leader	Can we cross, now?
Landowner	Now don't rush me! Let's see if you've achieved height order, first! (Using the help of the congregation the landowner now checks the volunteers are in height order.)
Leader	Now can we cross?
Landowner	(suitable pause) No! One last task I want completed.
Leader	(by now desperate) Anything, so long as we can cross and sit down for a rest.
Landowner	I want you to get yourselves in intelligence order – with the cleverest at the front, and the least clever at the back! The same rules apply.

At this point much dismay should occur. The group may be able to achieve one move if, for instance, there is a doctor in the group, or someone else with a good post-graduate degree, but after that they will be stuck. They will probably dislike marking themselves down as the 'least clever' or indeed as 'most clever'. When the activity has irretrievably broken down the landowner should step in.

| Landowner | Just joking! It's OK! You don't have to do that task. You can come across the bridge. |

The group of volunteers now 'cross the bridge' and join the landowner, where they stay to conclude this activity.

 ☐ *Conclusion*

Begin to unravel the feelings and thoughts of those in the 'story'. Ask questions of the landowner, the leader, and the rest of the walking party. For example:

- How did you feel when you were asked to move into age order?
- How did you (ask obvious leaders in the group of volunteers) feel, knowing that you were unable to organize the rest of the group?
- How did the youngest/oldest feel at the front/back of the line?

- How did you feel when you were asked to move into height order?
- How did you (ask the congregation) feel when you could see things going wrong in height order, but you were unable to do anything to help?
- How did the shortest/tallest feel at the front/back of the line?
- How did you feel when you were asked to move into 'intelligence' order? (Spend some time on this question, exploring why it was so difficult to achieve.)

Allow as much time as possible to explore how people felt. Simply acknowledge their feelings, rather than make comments.

☐ *Comment*

The Gospel reading today gives us two parables about invitations to dinner, they are part of a series of three such parables Luke puts together. The first of these parables is about humility.

The scene is a formal dinner, on the Sabbath, in the home of a wealthy Pharisee. Jesus has been invited to the dinner, and he uses this occasion to both heal and to teach those present. Many of those present are his enemies, and they make this quite clear when first he heals a man who has dropsy, complaining he has broken the Law by healing someone on the Sabbath. So it is to this mixed audience that Jesus tells the parable of the Guests at the Wedding Banquet.

Imagine, says Jesus, after watching the way the guests have arrived at the Sabbath dinner, that you arrive early at a wedding banquet. Immediately you take up the best seat, as of right. Yet how foolish you will feel if someone more important comes in later and your host has to ask you to sit lower down the table. Whereas if you sit at the bottom of the table, your host may ask you to move up to the place of honour on the top table.

At this point we might imagine this is simply just a story, except that Jesus ends with the words:

> For all who exalt themselves will be humbled, and those who humble themselves will be exalted. (Luke 14.11)

Being humble is a precondition of repentance. Unless we are humble we are not ready to ask God's forgiveness. If we are still full of pride we cannot honestly ask God to forgive us our sin. Humility is one of the signs of a great Christian; it is also one of the hardest to achieve. It comes when we realize that others can achieve more than us, that others have more to offer than us, and ultimately when we realize how unworthy we are of all God has given us.

As we can see with our 'acted story' we have a long way to go to achieve true (not false) humility. First comes prayer to ask God to enable us to see ourselves as he sees us.

PROPER 18

Sunday between 4 and 10 September inclusive

Unless we pick up our cross we cannot be disciples. This week we explore what it means to pick up our cross, and decide whether or not sometimes we choose to avoid picking it up.

Jeremiah 18.1–11
Philemon 1–21
Luke 14.25–33

- Words for the guided meditation.
- Focus material: icons, flowers, statues, water, etc.
- Large pile of nails.
- Meditation music.

☐ *Starter*

Explore what it really means when Jesus says, 'Whoever does not carry the cross and follow me cannot be my disciple', by first creating a tranquil atmosphere suitable for meditation. Where possible move chairs or pews to create an open space, leaving some seats at the sides for those who cannot easily sit on the floor. Form focus areas using water, statues, flowers, icons, and in particular a very large heap of nails. Ensure everyone has something to focus on. Play suitably quiet music on an instrument provided the musician cannot be seen, or use a CD. Alternatively play and sing some suitable Taizé music. Ensure all this happens before anyone enters the church, and encourage a silent welcome for this service.

Allow the normal service to proceed until the time for the 'sermon slot', and then revert to the quiet (but without the music) that was achieved at the beginning of the service. You may need to give warning to parents of young children what is to happen, and encourage them to walk around with young children who may be fractious, and at the worst to step outside for a moment or two at this point. Ensure they feel welcome, but stress the importance of trying to achieve some silence today. Make sure there is a special time to include these children and their parents at some other point in the service.

Ask the congregation to spend a moment or two in silence, perhaps looking at some of the focus material, or closing their eyes, and to think about Jesus carrying his cross to the place of crucifixion. Inform them you will help them by conducting a guided meditation, then read the words slowly, allowing time for everyone to 'clothe the ideas with their own thoughts'. Leave pauses for thought at the end of each line. You will probably need to practise this beforehand.

Guided meditation

Jesus steps from the shade of the building into the burning sun . . .
He is bruised and cut from the beating he has received . . .
When did he last have any food or water . . .
The noise of the crowds is deafening . . .
Passers-by throw rubbish at him . . .
They jeer and mock him . . .
Jesus is going to his death . . .
How heavy is the weight of a huge cross . . .

Give time for everyone to 'come round', then quietly begin the Comment.

☐ *Comment*

Jesus calls us to follow him, to leave family and friends, and to take up our cross and follow him. For most of us the phrase 'take up our cross' doesn't mean what it would have meant to a first-century disciple. To those who lived in the time of the Roman empire, the word 'cross' conjured up a terrible image of torture, with which they were all too familiar.

To pick up one's cross meant the certainty of a dreadful death, with no reprieve. We have gained some idea of what that might have meant through our meditation, and it might help us now to gain an insight into what Jesus meant when he said 'Whoever does not carry the cross and follow me cannot be my disciple'. Jesus seems to assume everyone has some kind of cross to carry, and the Christian journey is always fraught with great difficulty.

Perhaps this says something about the way often our journey isn't difficult. It might lead us to wonder if we are really following Jesus, when our Christian life is so easy. Does this mean that we are called to a harder path, and we've been trying to avoid it? Does this mean that we've failed to pick up the cross, and neatly stepped round it to avoid its weight?

☐ *Conclusion*

Encourage everyone to think about a time in their lives when it has been difficult to be a Christian, e.g. looking after an awkward relative; living with a family member who has made it difficult to go to church; ridicule of their faith by a colleague or family member; or a period of ill health. These might be said to be the 'crosses' in their lives.

Children might like to explore with an adult periods of difficulty other people have had in their lives. Keep the difficulties to those found in the ordinary ups and downs in life, rather than exploring the life of some Christian super-hero.

When all have identified the crosses in their lives, encourage them to go forward and to pick up a nail for each 'cross', and to return to their seat. The nails should be taken home and kept as a meditation focus, to encourage everyone present to remember that unless we pick up our cross we cannot follow Jesus.

PROPER 19

Sunday between 11 and 17 September inclusive

The parable of the Lost Sheep is acted out to remind us of our responsibility in searching for those who have not heard the gospel of Jesus Christ.

Jeremiah 4.11–12, 22–28
1 Timothy 1.12–17
Luke 15.1–10

- Shepherd and optional costume, including staff.
- 100 pictures of sheep to be hidden.
- Person to hide one sheep.
- Script for shepherd.
- 2 people to count the sheep pictures.
- Blackboard and chalk.
- List of questions.

☐ *Starter*

Act out the parable of the Lost Sheep. Before the service photocopy 100 copies of the sheep picture on page 134. They do not need to be too large. Hide these sheep all around the church and outside if

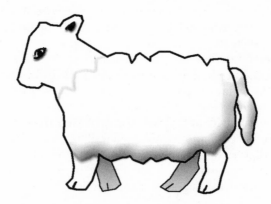

possible. It might be sensible to keep a list of where the sheep are placed, as this will make collecting them easier. Alternatively place stewards around, who know where the sheep have been placed. Make sure that one sheep cannot be found (perhaps by putting the picture into a book someone is holding).

Start by telling the background to the story of the Lost Sheep. If possible appoint someone else to do this, and invite them to 'think themselves into the story'. They might even like to dress up as a shepherd. The 'story' might go like this:

My name's Benjamin. It's my job to look after all the sheep from my village. I usually come up into the hills in the spring and pretty much stay up here. I work very much on my own, except when occasionally I see other shepherds up here, or someone from the village comes up.

I can tell our sheep because they're all known to me. See that one there, that's Old Man. I call him that because he's the oldest one in the flock. And that one, she's called 'Hawk', because when she was but a lamb she nearly got taken off by a hawk, but she struggled so much it let her go.

We wander the hills always trying to find the best bit of grass, and to avoid the worst places. There are some dreadful precipices up here. If you lose your footing you're done for! Many a time I've had to stop some sheep from straying too near the edge. Then there are the wolves. At night I gather the flock into a pen – we've got a number of walled pens on the mountains – and I sleep across the doorway to protect them. My staff has seen a number of battles with wolves over the years.

Anyway, I can't stand here chatting to you, it's time to gather the flock together and move back down the mountain. Winter's coming on! The rest of my fellow shepherds have already gone, I see. There'll be great rejoicing tonight when we all return safely.

(*Starts to move away, when struck with a thought.*)

I don't suppose you'd care to help me round up the sheep, would you? There's a hundred of them to find. They're not far away, should be all round here somewhere.

Everyone is encouraged, adults and children, to look for the sheep. Set up a 'sheep tally station' and give all the sheep to two people sitting at this station to count the numbers as they come in. A tally could also be kept on a large board for all to see. When the number reaches 99, stop. Re-count all the sheep if desired. When the number is still 99 call a halt to the activity. Hold a discussion about what to do next. Ask questions like:

- Have we searched every possible place?
- Are there any other places to look?
- Were there really 100 sheep to start with?
- Has another shepherd accidentally taken the sheep?
- How long should we go on searching? (Keep this in the present – How long has the service been already?)
- Should we give up?

Finally, resolve to have one more hunt. The shepherd could use phrases like, 'Where is my lost sheep?' and 'Have you found my lost sheep?' Send everyone out again, and then after a suitable time make sure the sheep is found. The person hiding the sheep could just pull it slightly out of the book when no-one is looking, and leave, ostensibly to hunt for the sheep. After a while someone else will spot the lost sheep. Make sure that a rousing shout is given!

 ☐ *Comment*

This parable is one of the most loved in our Bible. The image of the shepherd braving all kinds of danger to keep his flock safe, and continuing to search for his lost sheep long after it might be thought reasonable, is one known to us all.

We have discovered some of the issues involved for ourselves. When is it reasonable to stop looking? Has the sheep strayed into another flock? Were there really 100 sheep originally?

To the disciples this story would have had the immediacy of truth. It was based on a story which they had seen acted out each year of their lives. Shepherds gave their all to protect their flock, and if they failed then they at least brought back the fleece to show how the animal had died.

But of course this is a parable, and Jesus told this parable to many of those who were shocked by his lifestyle. He consorted with those who lived outside the Mosaic Law. These men and women did not obey the Jewish Law. They were unclean and any Jew who worked with them also put himself outside the Law.

The shepherd in the parable is God, and Jesus makes it clear that God welcomes all into his kingdom. No-one is considered beyond the pale! Indeed he leaves the rest of the flock (i.e. 'us') to go and find the lost sheep ('those outside the church'), and when the lost sheep is found there is such a welcoming party.

How much do we search for those who are lost, and how much do we welcome them into the church when they are found?

☐ *Conclusion*

Encourage the congregation to turn to their neighbour and talk about those in their neighbourhood (or work environment) who might be considered 'lost to the faith'. Choose someone or a group to pray for, and covenant with your neighbour to continue praying for this person or group until they can be considered 'found'. Alternatively, covenant to work with this person or group.

Centre the prayers for this service around evangelism and mission, praying for a specific group of people who might not have heard the gospel.

PROPER 20

Sunday between 18 and 24 September inclusive

As Christians we must remember that we cannot serve the world and God. Our first priority is to serve God.

Jeremiah 8.18—9.1
1 Timothy 2.1–7
Luke 16.1–13

> - Actors for one or both dramas.
> - Improvised scripts.
> - Desk.
> - 2 telephones.
> - Papers and a filing tray.
> - God and the World forms for everyone.
> - Pencils for everyone.

☐ *Starter*

Set up a piece of improvised drama. This will need careful working out and some rehearsal. Either produce one of the two pieces below, or both if time allows.

Role-play

Actors Two adults (a man and a woman) and three teenagers (either sex) or three adults acting as teenagers.

Story line 1 A couple win millions on the Lottery, but shortly afterwards separate. The money is divided between them. (One goes to stand on one side of the church, and the other on the opposite side.)

The couple have three children, over the age of 16 years, and each parent is concerned that they attract the support of the children against the other parent. They use the money to bribe the children separately and to bring them over onto 'their side'. The bribes need to clash with one another so the young people have great difficulty in choosing, and there is much discussion among them as to what they should do.

Examples of bribes offered by parents might be:

Parent 1   I've bought you a car (*name a make*), but you'll have to come over to France this weekend with me to collect it.

Parent 2   I've arranged to get tickets for the football international this weekend, but you'll have to come down Friday night so that we can travel to X (*name of venue*) on the Saturday.

Parent 1   I've bought a house for you to live in, in X (*name of a town*) so that you'll be able to accept the place at university after all.

Parent 2   I've arranged for you to stay in halls at X (*name of same town*), so you'll be able to enjoy all the fun at university this year. I know you really wanted to stay in college.

Parent 1   I've paid for a holiday for all three of you for next year in Malaga. I've booked the date for July 1st–14th, that was right, wasn't it?

Parent 2   I've paid for a holiday for all three of you for next year in Cyprus. I've booked the date for July 1st–14th, that was what you wanted, wasn't it?

Keep the discussions sensible, not allowing the problems to be resolved by simply giving facile answers. The three youngsters would like to stay on good terms with both parents. Make sure they are really torn between both parents, and cannot resolve the difficulties easily.

Role-play

Actors   Three adults

Story line 2   An office worker sits with his desk, two phones, filing trays and lots of paper. He is working very hard. At either side of the church are his two bosses. They constantly bombard him with requests over the phone, and in person. For example: 'Can you find X: I need it for a meeting now!' and 'Where are the minutes of the last board meeting, the chairman has asked for them!'

The pace hots up, but the office worker just about keeps everything working. He makes calls out to find information for one boss, while the other rings him, so he is on two phones at the same time. One boss wants him to take minutes, while the other wants him to go on a site visit, both at the same time.

Finally, have an absolutely impossible request from both bosses that cannot be negotiated away by the office worker. He can be accused of disloyalty and of not being supportive by one boss at this point. He finally collapses.

☐ *Comment*

Jesus taught his disciples they could not serve two masters at the same time. As we have seen, we get ourselves into impossible knots if we try to be fair to both of them. We simply cannot do our duty to two masters and keep our sanity.

But the purpose of this parable is to remind us that we cannot serve God and the world. If we put all our energies into the things of this world – into our job, our family life, our house – then we cannot give what is due to God. The hard truth is that God calls us to give him our first allegiance.

Second, if we get side-tracked by the glitter and glitz of the secular world we won't be able to see what it is God wants. We will be so dazed, we will have lost our clarity of vision. Only by keeping our gaze on God will we be able to discern what it is that he calls us to do in our lives.

☐ *Conclusion*

Before the service produce copies of the form below and pencils for everyone.

God and the World

In the past God and the World have clashed in my life, when:

....

In my life, now, God and the World have clashed when:

....

Allow time for people to sit quietly for a moment or two and to fill in their thoughts about where God and the World have clashed in their own lives. Encourage adults to help children.

PROPER 21

Sunday between 25 September and 10 October inclusive

The call to help others is continuous and we shall not be forgiven if we fail to notice those who need our aid.

Jeremiah 32.1–3a, 6–15
1 Timothy 6.6–19
Luke 16.19–31

- The Dramatized Bible.
- Bibles for all groups.
- Character Descriptions form for all groups.
- Actors: Judge, two barristers, Lazarus, and the rich man.
- Pens or pencils.

☐ *Starter*

Read the story of the rich man and Lazarus using the Dramatized Bible. Then divide the congregation into groups of ten adults and children. Invite each group to read the parable again. Next divide the group of ten people into two groups of five (Group A and Group B) and give each group a copy of the form below as well as a

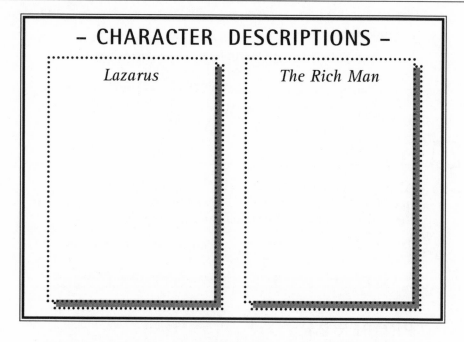

– CHARACTER DESCRIPTIONS –

Lazarus

The Rich Man

pen or pencil. Each group of ten will need a group leader, and these should probably be appointed the week before.

Group A is to look again at the parable from the view of Lazarus. What can they say about Lazarus and about the rich man? What kind of words would describe them? For example, Lazarus might be considered to be 'patient' or 'long-suffering', and the rich man might be thought of as 'callous'. Discuss both characters from Lazarus' perspective and then put down all that is possible on the form.

Group B is to look again at the parable from the rich man's point of view. What kind of words could be used to describe both men? Discuss both characters from the rich man's point of view, and then put down all that is possible on the form.

Bring groups A and B back together. With the help of the group leader to mediate, discuss both characters from the two different perspectives. What have they learnt? The forms are now passed to the service leader.

 ☐ *Conclusion*
Finally, set up a court scene with Moses as the mediator (or judge) between Lazarus and the rich man, and two barristers. This will need to have been worked on in the week before, but most of the help for the barristers should come from the different groups supporting the rich man or Lazarus. Their forms will provide ammunition for accusation and defence.

Start with Moses setting the scene of the action, outlining the case against the rich man, and finally announcing the rich man is appealing against an unjust ruling. He doesn't think he should be in hell! Lazarus then gives his story.

The two barristers take it in turns to accuse or defend their clients, using the information on the Character Descriptions forms. Finally Moses sums up and gives his verdict.

□   *Comment*

St Luke gives us another of his cameo pictures, this time a parable of two men, one rich and one poor. The language describes them exactly. The rich man is dressed in sumptuous clothing and his meals are a veritable banquet each day. Whereas Lazarus, the poor man, has been thrown down at his gate. The dogs lick his sores, and we should remember dogs are unclean, so this is the ultimate degradation.

The rich man must have seen Lazarus as he came and went, but he ignores him, not even throwing him the bread used to wipe his hands at table. When both die, his attitude continues. He begs Abraham to send Lazarus as though he were his servant, and he relies on being one of God's chosen people to get out of the hell he is in. He has learnt nothing, and Moses is unable to save him. The only sign that there is something good in him is the request to send someone to warn his brothers. But even here he is thwarted.

This parable is another strong warning about the need to use wealth wisely. We are only stewards of what we possess, and we are responsible for its use. To ignore the poor and wretched in our world is to act like the rich man ignoring Lazarus. We need to remember the other parable that Jesus told: 'It is easier for a camel to go through the eye of a needle than for someone who is rich to enter the kingdom of God' (Matthew 19.24). Helping to achieve fair trade around our world, or working for charities for the homeless, or raising money for the poor in third-world countries is not an optional extra. It is a demand upon all of us who live in relative luxury.

PROPER 22

Sunday between 2 and 8 October inclusive

Faith is something many Christians find difficult, yet we have faith in many of the things around us in our world.

Lamentations 1.1–6
2 Timothy 1.1–14
Luke 17.5–10

- Volunteers to play trust games.
- Copies of trust games for leaders.
- OHP or flip-chart.
- Fat felt-tip pen.

☐ *Starter*

Conduct one or two trust games, though do not use the word 'trust' when introducing them. Two examples are given below, but there are many more:

Knee sitting

Invite 12–15 people to volunteer to take part in this game. They should stand one behind the other, all facing the same way, in a very tight circle, and put their hands on the shoulders of the person in front of them. At a given moment invite them all to sit down slowly on the knees of the person behind them. Invite them to stand up and repeat the exercise at least twice more, particularly if it is not successful the first time. Point out that though no-one is sitting on a solid object, yet with trust in the person behind them they can sit down quite safely.

Human caterpillar

Invite a different group of volunteers to take part in this game. There should be at least 12–15 people who are reasonably agile. They should stand one behind the other, in a long line, with their hands *tight* round the waist of the person in front. When all are ready instruct them to bend their knees and lower themselves to the floor, into a position reminiscent of a Russian dancer. When this is achieved all should attempt to put their left leg and left shoulder forward, then their right leg and right

---

shoulder, so as to move slowly forward. An alternative to this would be not to bend down, but to try and walk together as a group. Make sure that people are not dragooned into this exercise as some will find it intimidating.

When the volunteers have returned to their seats debrief them on the exercises by asking questions like:

- Did you think the exercise would work?
- What were you thinking when you sat down/tried to walk forward?
- Were you surprised how easy/hard the exercise was?
- What made the exercise work?

□ *Conclusion*

Presupposing someone has mentioned the word 'trust' or 'faith' in connection with the games, continue by asking the congregation the question: 'How many things in your daily life do you have faith in?'

□ *Note*

Use either 'faith' or 'trust'.

Draw up a huge list of suggestions (e.g. 'that the sun will rise tomorrow', 'that *X* will cook dinner', 'that my house will stand firm against storms', etc.) and write them up on an OHP or flip-chart for all to see.

When the answers have dried up, ask the question: 'Why do you have faith in these things?' In other words, what are the characteristics of those things in which we put our trust and in which we have faith? One answer might be: 'they have never let us down yet', but there may be many more.

□ *Comment*

The disciples asked Jesus to give them more faith. Sometimes they must have felt helpless at the task before them, and at their own inability to carry out the work Jesus expected of them. There is a sense of desperation in the cry for help and in the quick answer they receive. Jesus says to them: 'If you had faith the size of a mustard seed, you could say to the mulberry tree, "Be uprooted and planted in the sea", and it would obey you' (Luke 17.6).

There is something incongruous in the notion of a mulberry tree growing in the sea, but nevertheless Jesus makes the point that with faith in God all things are possible. When we stop doing things in our own strength, and start to rely on God anything can happen. It might be thought an impossibility for a group to sit on each other's knees without someone actually sitting on something solid and safe, but as we now know it is possible if we have faith.

143

We have also seen that to have faith in something we need to believe we will not be let down. Jesus knew the only certainty in life was God. If we put our trust and hope in him, we will never be let down. So when life gets difficult, or when we believe we cannot do something, we need to remember we are not alone. With faith the size of a mustard seed we can achieve anything.

☐ *Note*

Include prayers for healing in this service.

PROPER 23

Sunday between 9 and 15 October inclusive

God gives us so much. Our response should be one of humble gratitude, but all too often we forget to return him our thanks.

Jeremiah 29.1, 4–7
2 Timothy 2.8–15
Luke 17.11–19

- Materials for leaf tiles: Plain flour, large quantities of salt, water, cooking oil, rolling pins, and leaves.
- Tables.
- Materials for leaf rubbing: Thin sheets of paper, card, scissors, leaves, wax crayons.
- Optional: Paint, chunky brushes (or sponges).
- Sufficient Count Your Blessings cards for all the congregation.
- Pencils.

☐ *Comment*

Our Gospel reading today is about the healing of the ten lepers. This miracle appears nowhere else in the Gospels; it is peculiar to Luke's Gospel. Jesus is on his way to Jerusalem, passing through the area of Samaria, when he is accosted from afar by ten lepers. 'Jesus, Master, have mercy on us!' they cry.

Such is their faith the lepers call Jesus 'Master', and start to hurry away to see the priest and register the fact they are cured, even before their cure is completed. But in due course it is only one leper who returns to thank Jesus, and he, we note, is a Samaritan. Do we have to infer the others were Jews? We don't know. But what we do know is this was the only one to return to show gratitude and praise to the person who had healed him.

It is all too easy to forget to say thank you to those who help us in our daily life, perhaps because they do so much for us. It is also easy to forget to thank God. Today we make a special point of thanking our family, our friends, our neighbours and God.

□ *Starter*

Explain that today everyone is to make something to take the *following week*, to give to someone as a 'thank you' present.

Encourage everyone to join either a leaf tile group or a leaf-rubbing group. The task of both groups is to make as many leaf tiles and as many leaf cards as possible, so there will be sufficient for all to take a tile and a card home the following week.

Leaf tiles
Ingredients
2 cups of plain flour, 1 cup salt, 1 cup water, 2 tablespoons cooking oil, a rolling pin, and a variety of leaves.

Method
1 Mix all the ingredients together to form a dough. Roll out with a rolling pin until the dough is 2 cm thick. The dough should be square or oblong and just a little larger than the leaf.
2 Take the leaf and press, vein-side down, onto the dough so it leaves a mark.
3 Remove the leaf and bake the dough in an oven later, for at least 2 hours at 130°C or 250°F or gas mark 1–2.

It would be better for one or two people to take the tiles home to bake. They can then be returned the next week for everyone to be given a tile. Make sure there are sufficient of a reasonable standard to be used as presents.

Leaf cards
Choose one of these two activities:
1 Before the service collect leaves of different shapes. Place the leaves under a thin sheet of paper and rub over them with a wax crayon. Cut round the rubbings and stick onto a folded piece of plain card.
2 Before the service collect a variety of leaves of all shapes and sizes. Put out two colours of paint and some chunky brushes on a suitable table. Paint one side of a leaf, where the veins

show most clearly. Alternatively use a sponge instead of a brush. When the leaf is covered with paint, place a piece of plain paper over it and smooth your hands across it to make a leaf print. When dry cut out and stick onto a folded piece of plain card.

☐ *Conclusion*

Before the service create a Count Your Blessings card for each member of the congregation.

Give out pencils and allow a few moments for everyone to think of one or two things for which they wish to thank God. Encourage them to take this home and use it as part of their prayers during the week.

PROPER 24

Sunday between 16 and 22 October inclusive

The message that we are to pray constantly and persistently if we are to be heard by God is used to look at our own prayer lives.

Jeremiah 31.27–34
2 Timothy 3.14—4.5
Luke 18.1–8

□ *Note*

This week follows the same subject as that in Proper 25, and can be used in tandem.

- Group leaders.
- Bibles.
- One or more large pictures of skeletons.
- Small Dry Bones cards.
- Materials for icon painting: 5 or 6 blocks of wood (2cm × 24cm × 14cm), sandpaper, powder paint, egg yolk, water if necessary, vinegar, brushes, small tins of model paint: gold, silver and copper.
- Prayer focus material, e.g. flowers, candle, picture.
- Different prayer books.
- Examples of subjects used regularly for Intercessions.
- Prayer Triptych cards for all members in the group.
- Pencils.

□ *Comment*

In the parable of the Widow and the Judge, St Luke gives us another of his brilliant portraits of two people in the Gospel reading today. The widow stands for all those who are poor and in need of care and nurture. The Law of Moses directs all Jews to care for those who are widowed, it is one of the primary duties of care. A judge would normally stand for all that is good about the Law. It is expected he would care for the weak and poor. However, in Luke's account he is shown as completely the opposite. He is unjust, and clearly a complete rogue. To be fair he may well not be a Jewish judge, since disputes were normally taken to the elders of the synagogue. It is probable he had been appointed by the Roman civil authority.

The widow appeals to the judge for justice against an opponent. She appeals not just once, but many times, until in the end the judge gives in to her demands. He realizes that he is never going to have a peaceful life unless he does as she asks, so he agrees to grant her justice.

Jesus commends the widow for her persistence. There was no way that she was going to give up this quest. She was like a dog with a bone! This, he says, is how we should be in our prayer life. We should continue at all costs, never giving up, and never losing heart. God will grant justice to his people who cry to him day and night.

□ *Starter*

In the week before the service appoint leaders to run the workshops. Set up four workshops, and any number of duplicates of these. Encourage the congregation to join whichever workshop attracts them. It might be helpful to put up large notices describing each workshop, so that people can decide which they would prefer to join.

□ *Workshops*

Meditation

Before the service create one or more large skeleton pictures (see page 149) with the words 'Dry Bones' below it (them), and place somewhere for all to see. The picture(s) will be used by a number of groups. Read Ezekiel 37.1–10. Talk about the passage for a moment. The words are specifically addressed to Israel, but the group might well be able to identify areas of their own life which feel dry or barren. These will be areas left uncultivated for some time, e.g. work, worship, friends, family, etc. If desired discuss these areas in twos rather than in the group. Finally give each person a small card with the picture of the skeleton on it, and invite them to make resolutions as to how they are going to change this situation. Write these resolutions onto the card.

Drama

Using the same picture of the skeleton as a focus, read the story of the dry bones from Ezekiel 37.1–10. Discuss the story with the group. Ask questions like: Who are the dead bones? What is wrong with them (physically and metaphorically)? Have you ever felt as though you were like this, spiritually? Are there areas in your life which are dry (e.g. work, worship, friends, family, etc.)? Finally create some mime to accompany the reading of the story.

Prayer

Talk about the times, the places, and the positions the group use for prayer: Do they only pray at night, or during the day? Do they get on their knees? Do they close their eyes? Do they have a set time

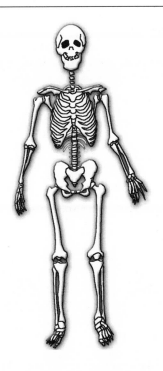

each day? What books do people find helpful for their prayers?
Finally, provide some suitable focus material and try out different
prayer positions (e.g. standing, sitting, kneeling, lying, arms raised,
open palms, etc.). If you are somewhere quiet, this could be
accompanied by suitable music. Give the group a topic for prayer,
or allow them to use this time to concentrate on their own personal
concerns. Finally, discuss how each position felt.

Icon
This workshop will only be possible if some preparation work is
carried out. Prepare five or six blocks of wood, that are 2cm thick
and at least 24cm by 14cm. Rub the wood down with sandpaper.
Prepare the paint beforehand by mixing together powder paint
with the yolk of an egg, a little vinegar, and some water if
necessary. The paint should be thick enough for the different
colours not to run into each other when they are wet. You will also
need some small tins of gold, silver and copper model paint, and a
variety of brushes. Create a border around the edge of the block,
which members can paint in dark red. Copy an existing icon(s)
which can be put up before the group. Lightly mark the outline of
the drawing in pencil, leaving group members to fill in the outline.
The whole block of wood should be painted. Allow only a small
number of people in the group. They could work together in twos,
and they should work in silence. The icons may well need

completing at a later stage by the addition of touches of gold, silver or bronze paint, sequins, and other decorations. Point out that icons are normally only started after a period of prayer, and start with a prayer.

Church Intercessions

This group should look at the pattern of Intercessions used in public worship in the church over the last year. Explore the style, the kinds of petition (which parts of the world get regularly prayed for?), and the books used. If possible collect as many different kinds of prayer books as possible and allow people to explore them. If lay people conduct the Intercessions do they get any training? If not, what kind of training might be helpful? If no lay people are used to lead Intercessions could this be set up? Would there be any volunteers from the group? Finally read the words of the Gospel again and discuss. Remembering Jesus advocates persistence in prayer, how could this be applied to our public prayers? Is there some way of keeping the prayer going each week, and checking periodically the results of the prayer? (Churches prayed for South Africa and for the Berlin Wall for many years, but things did eventually change!)

Prayer covenanting

Read the Gospel story again and discuss its meaning. Jesus advocates persistence in prayer. Talk about how we might persist in our personal prayer life: for example, establish a routine time and

~ *Prayer Triptych* ~

Ann, Mary and David
promise to pray for:

Colombia
Africa
Ireland

each weekday at 12 o'clock

place; use a prayer diary; or use church or diocesan Intercessions lists. Listen to group members' experiences, and the woes and joys of their prayer life. Finally, divide into threes, discuss what issues they might wish to pray for regularly and then agree to pray for them at specific times or days. Agree to meet monthly, if only for a few moments perhaps after worship, to review the subjects for which they are praying, and to take on more subjects if desired. Make a point of hearing from some of these groups annually. Give each group a Prayer Triptych card (see above) for them to record the time, day, and subjects for prayer.

☐ *Conclusion*

Hear back from all the groups, watch the drama, and look at the icons. Put up work so that everyone can also see it after the service.

PROPER 25

Sunday between 23 and 29 October inclusive

The right attitude to God is as important as persistence in prayer, if we are to be acceptable to him.

Joel 2.23–32
2 Timothy 4.6–8, 16–18
Luke 18.9–14

☐ *Note*

This week follows the same subject as Proper 24, and can be used in tandem.

- OHP or flip-chart and fat felt-tip pen.
- Oval stones for all the congregation.
- A paddling pool, baby's bath, or preserving pan, filled with water.
- Large number of cloths for drying the stones.
- Acrylic paint.
- Brushes.
- CD player, and suitable CD of meditative music.

□ *Starter*

Before the service place two or three large piles of smooth, oval stones somewhere very visible. In another corner of the church put a large container half-filled with water, for example, a toddler's paddling pool, a baby's bath or a preserving pan, depending on the size of the congregation and the number of stones needed. Put out as many old (or covered) tables as you can accommodate, and cover as much as possible of the floor around them with plastic.

Start by spending a few moments drawing up a master list of sins, and writing these up on an OHP or flip-chart, in order to help people identify their own sins.

When this is finished play some quiet music, and ask everyone to think about their own lives, concentrating on one or two sins which they have committed recently.

When people are ready they should be encouraged to go and fetch a stone (a symbol of their sin), and to place it in the bowl of water (a symbol of cleansing and forgiveness), before returning to their seat. All this occurs in silence.

□ *Comment*

In another beautifully drawn picture St Luke gives us the story of the Pharisee and the tax-collector. Both are in the Temple at prayer, but their attitudes contrast enormously. The Pharisee has time to sneak a look at the tax-collector in the middle of his self-satisfying thoughts, and congratulate himself on his life. Outwardly he does all the Law demands of him. He fasts twice a week, and he gives away a tenth of all his income. But it's almost as though he is speaking to himself, rather than to God, even though he lifts his eyes to heaven.

On the other hand the tax-collector does not dare to come too near to the presence of God, and stands far off beating his breast. He knows that he has sinned, and is unworthy to come into God's Temple. As a Jew collecting taxes for the hated Romans, he has no illusions about himself. There is nothing else the tax-collector can say, but to acknowledge his sin before God.

The major difference between the two men is their attitude towards God. Although (as we saw last week) perseverance in prayer is very important, a right attitude in prayer is also vital. As sinners all we have to do is to repent and return to God to be accepted by him. There are no hoops we have to go through to be received back by him, it is sufficient to acknowledge our errors before God. So it is the tax-collector who, despite his sin, is granted mercy and acceptance. The Pharisee, despite all his outward show, is not reconciled to God.

□ *Conclusion*

Comment that everyone present has acknowledged their sin before God. They have also picked up the symbol of that sin (the stone), and placed it in the symbol of cleanliness (the water). But now there is something more everyone can do. They can turn the stone into a thing of beauty.

Encourage everyone to go and pick out a stone from the water, and to dry it on a piece of cloth. Think about an image which conjures up 'being free of sin': it might be a dove, a cross, a fish, or some other Christian image. Using a brush and *one* colour of acrylic paint, paint the image on the stone. The activity should be carried out in silence, except for the accompaniment of some quiet music.

When the prayer stones are finished, mark each one with a name. At a later date when the stones are dry, paint with varnish. The stones can then be taken home and used as a focus for daily prayer.

BIBLE SUNDAY (OR LAST AFTER TRINITY)

We are reminded of many wonderful stories to be found in our Bible this week, and encouraged to immerse ourselves in its pages again.

Isaiah 45.22–25
Romans 15.1–6
Luke 4.16–24

- A large number of picture stories cut up.
- Optional: Actors to produce tableaux.

□ *Starter*

Before the service find two or three people who can draw sufficiently adequately to create 'outline' pictures of as many Bible stories as possible. The pictures should be drawn onto an A4 sheet of paper, with six pictures to the page. Choose stories which are graphic. Any of the following would be suitable, but there are many more:
Stories suitable for pictures:

- Joseph: Genesis 37—47.
- Moses: Exodus 3—12.

The Story of the Good Samaritan

- Ruth: Ruth 1—4.
- Shadrach, Meshach, and Abednego: Daniel 3.8–30.
- Daniel in the lion's den: Daniel 6.
- The temptations: Luke 4.1–13.
- Jairus' daughter: Luke 8.41–56.
- The Good Samaritan: Luke 10.30–37.
- The parable of the Great Dinner: Luke 14.16–24.
- The Prodigal Son: Luke 15.11–32.
- Lazarus and Dives: Luke 16.19–31.
- Zacchaeus: Luke 19.1–10.

Each story should now be cut into six parts and shuffled. Create mixed-age groups of three or four people, and give each group a Bible story in picture form. Their task is to guess the story and to put the pictures into the correct order. As groups complete their picture story, shuffle them and give them to others. Keep some more difficult ones for those who find this easy.

□ *Optional*

Give everyone a completed story, minus one piece. This should be given to another group. Groups should put their story together as far as possible, and then try to find from another group the piece which is missing.

□ *Optional*

Before the service prepare a piece of static drama, in the shape of different tableaux, to tell three or four of the stories. Offer these to the congregation in a confused order, and ask them to identify the stories and put them in the correct order. Make sure at least one unusual and less well-known story is included.

□ *Comment*

Today is Bible Sunday and we have been exploring some of the different stories in our Bible. It's been a kind of 'end of year test'. We seem to have done very well (or not done very well!).

Our Bible is a whole library of books, of course. It includes history, poetry, songs, letters and stories. In church we tend only to hear a small portion of the Bible, and there are large sections we never read. So we need to do more reading on our own.

If there were some stories this morning unknown to you then how about going home and looking them up? You might need the help of a concordance ('a book that tells you where to look in the Bible for certain words or phrases') to find the stories. Or you might like someone to help you understand the text, since it is not always obvious at first sight.

You might try covenanting with another person to read a certain section during the week, and then spend a few moments discussing the passage. You could try reading the Bible aloud, particularly if there are children at home. Talk about the story and find out what you need to know to help you understand it better.

Whatever way you read your Bible, the important thing is that you keep reading. To learn more about God and about the way he wants us to live, we need to become truly immersed in his word.

□ *Conclusion*

Discuss with the congregation how many Bible stories they could identify, and which ones they found difficult. Which stories do they want to go home and read once more? Finally, see if any of the congregation would like to start a reading scheme, e.g. the Bible Reading Fellowship's *New Daylight* series.

THE FOURTH SUNDAY BEFORE ADVENT
Sunday between 30 October and 5 November inclusive

God reminds his people what he requires of them – they should change their lives and then come and worship him.

Isaiah 1.10–18
2 Thessalonians 1.1–4, (5–10), 11–12
Luke 19.1–10

- Paper and pencils, if desired.
- Group leaders, if desired.
- OHP or flip-chart and pen.
- Promise forms and pencils.

□ *Starter*

Divide the congregation into small mixed-age groups, and invite them to discuss 'What do we give to God?'

If desired give each group a piece of paper and a pencil, and appoint a group leader. If necessary start the discussion by offering any of the following as things we give to God:

- Prayer.
- Worship.
- Praise.

Allow time for the groups to explore the question in depth. For example: 'What does each age-group offer to God?'

Finally hold a plenary session. Put up all the suggestions on an OHP or flip-chart to create a master list of suggestions.

□   *Comment*

Isaiah speaks God's word to the people. He accuses them of behaving like the people of Sodom and Gomorrah and complains that God does not want sacrifices of blood. No matter how often they bring bulls, rams, or goats to offer to God, or how many festivals they observe, their offerings will not be acceptable. Such gestures, he says, are futile.

So what does God want from Israel? Isaiah says instead of pointless sacrifices, God wants his people to change their whole

My Promise

- **Stop gossiping**

- **Be nicer to my brother**

- **Visit my elderly neighbour regularly**

- **Be kinder to others**

- ●●●●●●●●●●●●●●●●●

lives. They should present themselves before God, free of all evil. He wants his people to care for each other, to seek justice for one another, to care for those who are poor, and to support the weak as well as those who cannot defend themselves.

In St Luke's Gospel the same message occurs. The people are amazed when Jesus decides to spend time in the house of Zacchaeus, and they grumble among themselves. Surely, they mutter, Jesus must know this man is a sinner. After all he is the chief tax-collector, a man who defrauds others, and a man who works for the hated Romans. How can a rabbi enter the house of such a man, when to do so is to break the Mosaic Law? But Jesus knows Zacchaeus has already seen the error of his ways, and has changed. He declares to the people: 'Today salvation has come to this house . . .' (Luke 19.9).

We offer to God many things, as we have already discovered. But all too often what we offer is not acceptable to God. We try to offer what we want to give him, and not what God actually wants. God doesn't want us to give him the equivalent of the Jewish sacrifice, that is, constant vigils, fasting, or even too much concern with the perfection of our worship. He simply wants us to change our ways. First, he wants us to change ourselves, and only then to come and offer him worship and praise.

□   *Conclusion*

Give each member of the congregation a blank promise form and a pencil, and invite them to make some promises to themselves and to God. The promises should be aimed at trying to change themselves and become more acceptable to God.

The promise forms should be re-evaluated in about eight weeks' time as part of the congregation's Advent preparation for Christmas.

THE THIRD SUNDAY BEFORE ADVENT
Sunday between 6 and 12 November inclusive

Everyone has to make a decision whether to choose good or evil in their life, to choose the things of God or the things of Satan.

Job 19.23–27a
2 Thessalonians 2.1–5, 13–17
Luke 20.27–38

- Sticks, paper, glue, and large felt-tip pens for flags.
- A secret group to meet before the service.
- Large sheets of paper.
- Fat felt-tip pens.
- Prit-tak or drawing pins.

□ *Starter*

Before the service create 8 or 16 flags (from small green garden canes, and coloured paper cut into a V shape and stuck onto the canes). Also before the service form a group of people who will carry out the same activity as the others, i.e. to persuade people to join their country, but this country will not appear attractive. This group should meet the week before the service to plan their campaign, but on the day the existence of the group is to remain secret until the other groups have given their displays. So members of this group will need to take part in other groups' work initially.

Divide the congregation into two or four groups, depending on the size of the congregation. Everyone should be involved if at all possible. Give the following information to each group, on a slip of paper:

You are all people of a country. It is a very special country, but there aren't very many people belonging to this country. In order to persuade everyone else your country is the best in the world, and they should join you, you should:
- Decide on the name of your country.
- Decide what is good about your country (geography, opportunities, climate, etc.).
- Decide what selling points you can use to persuade others to join you (you may offer some positive advantages, but use no bribery).
- Come up with a slogan to shout at the end of the presentation.
- Decide on one or two people who will put your case to the other groups and try to persuade them to join you.
After the name of the country has been decided, any children should write the name onto the flags provided. If necessary an adult could write the word and the children could colour them in. They may not have very long to do this, though.

When the groups have prepared their case, invite one group to speak to the others. Remind them their aim is to persuade other people to join them. Those listening should decide during the presentation whether they would like to join this country, and at the end all may move to another country.

When all the groups have finished, surprise them by informing them there is one more country they should hear from. Invite the secret group to speak. They should have prepared their case so that their country may appear superficially attractive, but there is always a sting in the tail, e.g. there are beautiful mountains but you need oxygen to live there; wonderfully attractive seaside beaches, but it floods badly and many have been drowned over the years; the law of the land states only young people can live in the land which makes it an exciting place to live, but it also means the elderly have to escape or are killed, etc. Have flags as with the other groups, and try to get people to join. Obviously no-one should want to join this group.

Finally, invite the whole congregation to go to the country they would prefer. Hopefully there will be some movement.

□   *Comment*

St Paul's letter to the Thessalonians (we will presume it was written by St Paul) indicates they have written to him in a rather nervous state of mind. They are worried they are going to be tested, and the Second Coming of Christ is about to happen. Because of what Jesus had taught his disciples, they were obviously expecting a time of great violence, a battle between good and evil, leading to some cataclysmic horror. If this were to happen, they believed their faith would not be strong enough to stand the test.

Paul cleverly does not push them further than they can go at present, by agreeing they may not have enough faith. Instead he bolsters their fragile confidence as much as he can. He also disagrees that the Day of the Lord (the name for this event) has actually come. He argues there is much that will happen before this occurs. First will come a rebellion against God, and the power of evil will continue to grow, he says, before the final battle between God and Satan when evil will be defeated.

As Paul knew there is a force for evil in the world and many men and women are attracted to it, and turn away from all that is good. We might think this is an easy decision to make, but as we have just seen it isn't quite so easy. Most of us (or all of us) chose to support the country which gave us the best advantages, and few (or none of us) chose the country that offered us such less appealing advantages. The last country seemed attractive initially, but in each case the attractive advantage had a sting in the tail.

Yet all too many people in our world choose the attractive package and prefer not to see the sting in the tail. For the things of Satan can seem very attractive initially. So they choose the superficial attractiveness of the things of this world which lead nowhere, over the attractiveness of the things of God which lead to joys unimaginable. One choice we all have to make is whether we are on God's side or Satan's.

☐ *Conclusion*

Gather the groups together again and invite them to spend a few moments thinking about how to 'sell' Christianity, in the way they were selling their imagined countries. What good points can be brought out? What slogans used? How best can it be put over to people?

Give each group a large sheet of paper and a fat felt-tip pen and ask them to come up with some suggestions.

Finally put up the solutions around the church, and if there is time ask speakers to go through the points. Can any of them be put into practice in your church?

THE SECOND SUNDAY BEFORE ADVENT

Sunday between 13 and 19 November inclusive

A study of our hands and how we use them helps Christians to think about the way they should live their lives.

Malachi 4.1–2a
2 Thessalonians 3.6–13
Luke 21.5–19

- A picture of a pair of hands.
- OHP or flip-chart.
- Newspapers or magazines.
- Scissors.
- Prit-tak.

☐ *Starter*

Before the service create some focus material in the shape of a pair of hands. This could be on an OHP or flip-chart.

Divide the congregation into small groups of 2–4 people with instructions to examine their own and their neighbour's hands, according to the following categories:

- Caring hands.
- Working hands.
- Loving hands.

After everyone has examined their own and their neighbour's hands, they should decide what kind of care or work they think each pair of hands customarily carries out during the week. If people know one another, they may be able to guess some answers (e.g. 'Cares for sick husband', or 'Does the gardening'). It may also be that some people fit into all three categories.

The groups will have identified many positive uses for our hands, but now invite them to think about the way people use their hands in a negative fashion. What evil things do we do with our hands? (e.g. hit someone; shake a fist; create weapons; smash something.) The groups might also want to look at the wider picture of how we have used our hands to destroy our world in the last century.

Hold a plenary session, if desired, and gather the groups' conclusions together. These could be put up on an OHP or flip-chart, or alternatively used later during the conclusion of this section of the service.

□ *Comment*

In the Epistle reading, we see St Paul exhorting the Thessalonian Christians to keep away from those believers who are living in idleness. He admonishes them to follow the example he and Timothy gave them when they stayed with them in Thessalonica. While there they worked for their food, paying for everything they ate, in order to set an example to others. St Paul is concerned that now there are Christians who live in idleness, and who do not do their fair share of work. He urges them to change their ways, and begin to live according to the example they were set.

We know St Paul worked as a tent-maker while at the same time travelling throughout modern-day Turkey and Greece, teaching people about Jesus and setting up new churches. His hands were kept busy even while he talked. He was never idle.

We have been looking at our hands, and at all the useful ways that we use them. Our hands can also lead us into sin, either because we use them wrongly or through idleness. We can hurt others in all kinds of different ways through the use of our hands. We need to remember that there is always a choice.

□ *Conclusion*

Create a collage, using pictures from newspapers or magazines, to show all that is good and positive about the use of our hands.

Alternatively, produce some mime to demonstrate the use of our hands. This could be put to a poem or piece of prose about hands.

CHRIST THE KING
Sunday between 20 and 23 November inclusive

God works with those who act as faithful shepherds to his people. Sometimes these are kings and sometimes prophets.

Jeremiah 23.1–6
Colossians 1.11–20
Luke 23.33–43

- Bibles.
- List of kings for every group.
- OHP or flip-chart.

□ *Comment*

Jeremiah reminds his listeners a time will be coming when God will bring in changes. He has seen the way his people are scattered and neglected, and he intends to bring his people back together and give them shepherds who will care for them and nurture them.

God will honour his promise to his people. Israel had broken their promise with God, and for this rebellion they had been judged. However, God intends to gather his people back from the places where they had been exiled, and honour the promise made by Nathan to David (see 2 Samuel 7.11b–16). Here Nathan sees David as the first of a long dynasty of rulers.

Judah and Israel, the two divided kingdoms, are both included in this prophecy. From the line of David is to come 'a righteous Branch'. In other words the royal line of David is not dead, and it will flower again under a legitimate king. This future king will be the ideal king who will rule his people with justice. This king we identify with Jesus – born of the house of David!

□ *Starter*

As we have heard, Jeremiah says that God intends to install faithful shepherds to care for his people. He doesn't specify if these shepherds are to be prophets or kings, though if the latter not many seem to fit this criterion of faithfulness. Discuss what Jeremiah might mean by 'faithful shepherd'. For example, King David would have been considered a faithful shepherd of his people. However, he certainly sinned (i.e. see Bathsheba and Uriah, the Hittite). What criteria will you use to decide if the prophets or kings are faithful or not?

Then carry out a study of both kings and prophets in the Old Testament to see if the congregation can determine which, if any, can be said to be 'faithful shepherds' of their people. Either start the search from Jeremiah and go forward, or start further back with King Saul.

Give out as many modern Bibles to the congregation as possible. They can be any edition. Encourage them to work in twos or threes, and allocate different kings/prophets to different groups. It will not matter if some groups work on the same people as some of the stories are long. You might divide up some of the longer sections again. Their task is to find 'faithful shepherds'. In each case they are to give reasons for their choice, or for their rejection (e.g. 'King Jeroboam was an evil king because . . .'). Note that sometimes kings' names are changed slightly, which can cause confusion. Also, look up the books written by the prophets if there is no Bible reference.

ISRAEL

Prophet	King
Samuel	Saul
Book of Samuel	1 Samuel 9–31
	Ishbaal
	2 Samuel 2.8—4.8
Nathan	David
2 Samuel 7—12	2 Samuel 5—1 Kings 2.11
	Solomon
	1 Kings 2.11—11.43

NORTHERN KINGDOM (Israel)		SOUTHERN KINGDOM (Judah)	
Prophet	King	Prophet	King
	Jeroboam		Rehoboam
	1 Kings 11.26—14.20		1 Kings 11.43—14.31
	Nadab		Abijam
	1 Kings 15.25–28		1 Kings 15.1–8
	Jehu		
	1 Kings 16.1–7, 11–13		
	Baasha		Asa
	1 Kings 15.27—16.6		1 Kings 15.8–24
	Elah		
	1 Kings 16.6–10		
	Zimri		
	1 Kings 16.9–20		
	Tibni		
	1 Kings 16.21–22		
	Omri		
	1 Kings 16.21–28		
Elijah	Ahab		Jeohoshaphat
1 Kings 17	1 Kings 16.28—22.40		1 Kings 22.1–50

2 Kings 2.11	Ahaziah 1 Kings 22.40—2 Kings 1.18		Jehoram 2 Kings 8.16—25
Elisha 1 Kings 19.16 2 Kings 2—13.21	Jehoram 2 Kings 1.17, 2 Kings 9.14-24		Ahaziah 2 Kings 8.25—9.27
	Jehu 2 Kings 9.2—10.35		Athaliah 2 Kings 11.1-16
	Jehoahaz 2 Kings 10.35, 13.1-9		* Jehoash 2 Kings 11.2-12.21
	* Joash 2 Kings 13.9-13, 14.8-16		Amaziah 2 Kings 14.1-9
Jonah	Jeroboam II 2 Kings 13—14.29	Isaiah	Azariah 2 Kings 14.21-22
Amos	Zechariah 2 Kings 14.29—15.10	Micah	
Hosiah	Shallum 2 Kings 15.10-15	Obadiah	
	Menahem 2 Kings 15.14-22		
	Pekahiah 2 Kings 15.23-26		
	Jotham 2 Kings 15.5, 32-38		
	Pekah 2 Kings 15.25-28		Ahaz 2 Kings 16.1-20
	Hoshea 2 Kings 17.1-4	Isaiah 2 Kings 20	Hezekiah 2 Kings 16.20

Fall of Northern Kingdom

Prophet	King
Nahum	
	Manasseh 2 Kings 21.1-18
	Amon 2 Kings 21.18-26
Jeremiah	Josiah 2 Kings 22.1—23.30
Habakkuk	
Zephaniah	Jehoahaz 2 Kings 23.31-34

The Exile

Prophet	King
Daniel	Jehoiakim 2 Kings 23.34—24.6
	Jehoiachin 2 Kings 24.6
Ezekiel	Zedekiah 2 Kings 24.17—25.7

The Restoration

Prophet	King
Zechariah	
Haggai	
Malachi	

* Sometimes called Joash or Jehoash

□ *Optional*

Read Bible stories to the children about some of the kings or prophets who might be considered to have obeyed God for much of their lives.

□ *Conclusion*

Gather the information together and put onto an OHP or flip-chart to show those who might be considered to be faithful shepherds of God's people, and those who are not. Allow discussion if there is disagreement over choices.

The Society for Promoting Christian Knowledge (SPCK) was founded in 1698. Its mission statement is:

To promote Christian knowledge by

- **Communicating the Christian faith in its rich diversity**

- **Helping people to understand the Christian faith and to develop their personal faith; and**

- **Equipping Christians for mission and ministry**

SPCK Worldwide serves the Church through Christian literature and communication projects in 100 countries, and provides books for those training for ministry in many parts of the developing world. This worldwide service depends upon the generosity of others and all gifts are spent wholly on ministry programmes, without deductions.

SPCK Bookshops support the life of the Christian community by making available a full range of Christian literature and other resources, providing support for those training for ministry, and assisting bookstalls and book agents throughout the UK.

SPCK Publishing produces Christian books and resources, covering a wide range of inspirational, pastoral, practical and academic subjects. Authors are drawn from many different Christian traditions, and publications aim to meet the needs of a wide variety of readers in the UK and throughout the world.

The Society does not necessarily endorse the individual views contained in its publications, but hopes they stimulate readers to think about and further develop their Christian faith.

For information about the Society, visit our website at *www.spck.org.uk*, or write to:
SPCK, Holy Trinity Church, Marylebone Road,
London NW1 4DU, United Kingdom.